Enjoy me

In the Wake of the Raj:
Travels in 1950s India

⬗◆⬖

Desmond Higgins

Desmond Higgins   *October 2014*

Third Edition

Published by

MELROSE BOOKS

An Imprint of Melrose Press Limited
St Thomas Place, Ely
Cambridgeshire
CB7 4GG, UK
www.melrosebooks.com

THIRD EDITION 2011

Cover designed by Matt Stephens

ISBN 978-1-907732-34-8

FSC
www.fsc.org
MIX
Paper from
responsible sources
FSC® C013604

Printed and bound in Great Britain by:
CPI Group (UK) Ltd, Croydon, CR0 4YY

CONTENTS

PREFACE

Today, cheap flights make India very accessible. Previously, in their non air-conditioned ships, the wealthy booked 'Port Out, Starboard Home' to avoid the heat. 'Posh' thus entered the English language.

It is comforting to note that Indians sometimes express concern for the predicaments of westerners. An American adviser in a village was using enlarged pictures of mosquitos to illustrate their dangers. Astounded by the apparent size of the 'American' mosquito, they commiserated with the expert because as the Indian mosquito seldom exceeded ¼ inch in length, the villagers' problems were negligible by comparison.

These scribblings were penned at the end of the 1950s with little subsequent editing. Hence, where prices are shown I have not attempted to translate them into today's values. The place names are those of the 1950s.

I invite the reader to forgive or ignore the indiscriminate use of the first, second and third persons, singular and plural, throughout the script.

My thanks to Indians who made my sojourn with them so memorable and enjoyable.

My apologies to the people of south India for not qualifying the title.

The reader might care to note that the India of the 1950s had a population of 400 million. Today, that figure is in excess of 1,000 million.

P.S. As a junior diplomat on his first posting, I arrived in India in November 1957. From the tiny school I was associated with they marked my departure with a serenade:

> Goodbye Mr Higgins,
> We're sorry you must go.
> You gave our school a splendid start
> And helped to make it grow.
> We give you our good wishes
> To speed you on your way,
> And hope that we'll be seeing you
> Again one happy day.

My return to India, alas, was as a retiree almost exactly 50 years later to the day in November 2007. I found a land with three times the population that I had left. India now counts 1.2 billion people, growing by 20 million each year. Yet the general standard of living is higher. An imperfect barometer of worldly wealth is demonstrated by the higher proportion of brick-built to mud houses now to be seen in the countryside. The countryside itself is disappearing as construction of factories and homes grows apace.

Intense poverty is still evident everywhere. Road travel is chaotic and observance of traffic lights appears advisory, not obligatory. At one point, our driver, seeing that the traffic coming towards us on the other carriageway was lighter, chose to travel against the flow. We survived.

For today's visitor, hotels have replaced rest houses and the standards in many cases put Europe's in the shade. Since hotel employment is treasured, courtesy and helpfulness are everywhere.

Nonetheless, although hygiene standards for the visitor are enormously improved, I remained sufficiently cautious to follow an old habit: a tot of whisky each morning before brushing my teeth to keep stomach problems at bay.

With industry spreading haphazardly, it struck me that India is in the developmental stage that was evident in Spain 40 years ago. Except for the poverty, India is indeed a changed and better country than I knew 50 years previously. I wish her people well.

Desmond Higgins October 2008

Dedicated to my granddaughters
Natasha, Lara, Suzy and Katriana

CHAPTER 1

ARRIVING

Look! There's the Taj Mahal.

From the ship entering harbour you can see Bombay's mighty hotel, which was built in error facing inland rather than seaward, as the designer had planned. He committed suicide on discovering the irreparable mistake.

To the westerner arriving in Bombay for the first time, the contrast between the real thing and the pictures drawn in the imagination is striking. To ask new arrivals for their first impressions is to receive replies remarkable and commonplace. The majority are so overwrought by the turmoil of arrival and apprehension that nothing at all registers, except perhaps a feeling of homesickness. It is clear – and unflattering to India – that most people think in terms of dirt, beggars and holy men. Bombay is the aspiration of many Indian city and town dwellers; Delhi, the capital, is regarded by many of the upper class – particularly Bombay and Calcutta wallas – as being as isolated as Canberra is to Australian affairs. Despite the westernisation of the city, Bombay gives one some impressions. It is not dirt that abounds; cows are not to be found in the profusion one imagined, although they do appear; the number of beggars fades into insignificance against the great mass of ordinary Indians; and 'holy men' have a thin time in the typical city atmosphere.

But in the heat, which is all enveloping, the smells contain a peculiar twang; it is not offensive. Indeed, one meets it only when passing the food shops, and it is never so repugnant to the nostrils as the dirt and squalor of parts of southern Italy. Dilapidation is the keynote of everything, not dirt, for everything has to last so much longer in India; Indians cannot afford the luxury of discarding an asset so long as it will conceivably serve any purpose. Hence the buildings one sees are on their last legs by any Western standards, but they serve the purposes of housing and offices, for they are unable to substitute new for old. Whether one examines the Marine Drive, or any other road in Bombay, or the buildings, the vehicles – from bicycles to buses – or the clothing of the populace, the newly arrived westerner is struck by this all-embracing dilapidation. But to Indian eyes, Bombay is the essence of Western refinement. Yet there is something else that marks the place off from the west – it is in the lack of drabness, the secret of which is sunshine, hot and wearying though it may be.

Bombay, goes the trite remark, is not India. Nor for that matter is Calcutta or Delhi, or the country's fourth city, Madras. But like most generalisations, it does not stand examination. This is particularly true in regard to Delhi in the hot north of the country, 1,000 miles from any of the other three main cities and on the road to nowhere, as many Indians, particularly those from the non-Hindu speaking south, will testify. However, it is India's capital, although its central position has been affected by the creation of Pakistan. In grandeur there is nothing to equal it. New Delhi was built as the political capital in the 1920s after a site to the north of Delhi had been rejected at the last moment because of the mosquito menace. The lavish Whitehall of India – the huge secretariat blocks – the ceremonial way in the form of the Rajpath (meaning King's Way), soon to be flanked by gracious government offices, and at the end of the Rajpath is the Buckingham Palace of India – the President's Palace. All this grandeur is fitting for any sovereign state. The Rajpath provides one of the world's most impressive display grounds for ceremonial occasions. The one unfortunate siting is the Parliament building, which is circular and known by the unkind epithet of 'The Monkey House'. It is located in isolation from the main plan, which is a pity, for it is itself an impressive building. It caters for both Upper and Lower Houses of Parliament – the Rajya Sabha and Lok Sabha. Indeed, the chambers of the two houses have the unique distinction throughout the Commonwealth of being semi-circular in shape and not rectangular, as at Westminster and elsewhere. Inside the Parliament building is another huge hall – the chamber in which the Constitution was inaugurated and in which the Constituent

Assembly met. It is gradually being adorned by the portraits of the great men of independent India. If pressed, your guide will explain the electronic voting system in the chambers: there are two buttons that must be pressed simultaneously, one by each hand, in order to record a yea or nay vote, and they are sited on each MP's desk in such a way that he cannot surreptitiously lean over and record an extra vote from his neighbour's empty seat!

New Delhi in the 1920s was good shooting country. Today, not only have public buildings been erected, but palatial houses for senior officials too. One of the tasks of Indian Government officials is the provision of accommodation for all levels of staff – although with the expansion of Government services there are long waiting lists. The bigger houses have large gardens and these are severely criticised by junior civil servants who have to come from afar. In most cities, one finds the wealthier classes further out of town, whilst the poorer are crammed into the centre and, of course, near their place of work. New Delhi reveals the opposite, but the time will surely come when blocks of flats appear in the select gardens of New Delhi to house the rapidly growing population. As it is, the civil servants cycle in from the outlying colonies, come rain, hail or snow, although little of the latter two will bother Delhi. The rain similarly does not bother the cyclists, who do not have the cash to buy raincoats, for instead of putting on a covering garment – although some of the more affluent will wrap a piece of plastic sheeting round them – they will take off most of their clothes. And so in the monsoon you will see hordes of gentlemen cycling around in their 'underpants' with the remainder of their garments tied in a bundle underneath the saddle – all very ingenious and enterprising and no doubt healthy. Of course, ten minutes later in their offices they are immaculately clothed again and glowing with the soaking they have just had!

The rains in Delhi do graver things – either there are floods and there is too much water, or there is too much water and not a drop to drink. This happened recently when the terrific volume of water in the river scoured a new channel for itself, thus by-passing the waterworks! The army had to be called in to make a diversion channel at great speed to quench the rabid thirst of Delhi. But to some of Delhi's residents the rains are a blessing, for they mean that any old street will contain a puddle, and thus it is not necessary to trek long distances with heavy pitchers to collect water. I will not vouch for the hygienic qualities of water thus collected, but it is time and labour saving.

Delhi's municipality has a big job – not only must it develop building sites and keep them tidy, but it must also knock down unofficial dwellings. Living close to one's place of employment has an attraction not limited to the West. In India, although do-it-yourself kits are not in evidence, the craze extends itself to the construction of houses through sheer necessity. The purchased items are bricks and a strip of matting to lay across the top – probably costing £2 in all. The labour is provided by the would-be owner, and all is well until the municipality appear and knock down the 'unauthorised' dwelling. The only saving grace is that the replacement home will be up again within 24 hours.

Within sight of many of these colonies, the new embassies and high commissions of the diplomatic corps are rising. In the Chanakyapuri area, known as the Diplomatic Enclave, new buildings are going up, reflecting the styles of the home country or something that is allegedly a blend of East and West. They are all at it – Russians and Americans, Chinese and British, French and Vietnamese. On a slight rise overlooking all is the mighty Ashoka Hotel, the representative of the New India. In this international contest, for contest it is, the blocks of flats for staff of the United Kingdom mission are perhaps the most advanced and may prove to be the prototype for Indian housing of the future. Here I must point out that the ideal Indian home is that built with thick walls, few windows, and hence rather dim inside, with wide shaded verandahs and high ceilings. It would face west and east away from the noonday sun. But the architects of these British flats have faced the picture windows in the main rooms south and north on the principle that during summer the sun is too high in the sky to enter southern aspect windows, but would enter east and west aspect windows morning and evening. Yet in winter the sun is low enough in the sky to enter south-facing windows, giving much-needed warmth to the home – a north Indian middle-class house is like a refrigerator in the winter months. When this scheme is allied with air conditioning throughout, there is little need for expensive verandahs and space is thus saved. There is but one snag to this: in India light means heat and it is still necessary to darken a room to reduce the temperature, and your electricity bill. But please do not view these buildings from the Ridge overlooking Delhi, as I did, to hear an Indian enquire of the British High Commission flats: "What are they – the servants' quarters of the Ashoka Hotel?"

Delhi is essentially a provincial city; it has none of the great suburban train network of Bombay or Calcutta, which is an inevitable accoutrement of Western cities, even those with much smaller populations. It has expanded rapidly, but not in the proportions one would envisage, for the incoming refugees and work-seekers have merely crowded into the heart of the old city. There they live in incredible conditions, with their charpoys (string beds) leaning against the walls in daylight and then laid out in the roadway by night, or on the rooftops. For whatever you might be told about the frightful heat in the daytime, it does not freeze at night, and it is far more pleasant and healthy to sleep out of doors. Indeed, in the suburban gardens at about nine o'clock on any evening you will see the bearer bring out the charpoys and line them up on the grass for occupation by all the members of the household. In the early morning just before sunrise, the ladies of the household will nip inside to resume their sleep so that they will not be seen in bed by the neighbours over the garden walls.

Old Delhi abounds with the remains of British rule: of the troubles of 1857, of the lives of the British community in the late 19th century. In the clubs, in the houses, in the monuments and relics of this part of the city, now strangely lacking in activity though by no means deserted, the ghosts of former days are there. Take the Roshanara Club with its cricket ground and tennis courts, surrounded by trees, with its bearers serving drinks in the lounge whose walls are hung with the portraits of former chairmen, all English, severe looking and imparting a note of awe and a need for silence around the place. And quiet it is, as the servants pad about in bare feet and on Saturday nights go in fear of getting a minimum of one toe crushed by the dancers doing that most popular of dances, the samba, otherwise known as the Sikh's shuffle. Over the great mantelpiece in the bar is displayed the club's motto, or perhaps the moral of the club: 'Work is the downfall of the drinking classes'. But what could be nicer than to sit on the lawn, serenely lit by a few lamps, in the still warm evening and drink the drink of the expatriate, knowing that – for some curious reason – the temperature here is at least ten degrees lower than in New Delhi?

The American visitor invariably pays a visit to the Mutiny Memorial, a memorial to the British soldiers who were killed in the 1857 revolt. This is listed in the guidebooks as a must, and the intrigued American never ceases to wonder at the inclusion in the tourists' round of a monument which commemorates those who died in their efforts to stamp out the Indians' First War of Independence. At this point you get a good view of Delhi, and you can hear a good deal of Delhi; not the perpetual drone of cars and the like, but the noise of thousands of voices mingling together coming up from the heart of the city beneath. The area from which this perpetual buzz rises is the Covent Garden of Delhi, known quite logically as Subzi Mandi (vegetable market), which works on much the same principle as Covent Garden. Hordes of vehicles rush through the night with their loads of cabbages, tomatoes and the rest of it. But the mode of transport varies somewhat, for the vehicles that come to an abrupt halt in Delhi's Subzi Mandi are bullock carts. They start their journey about 24 hours previously – hundreds of them – from the outlying villages. Sleep for the drivers is secured en route, merely by letting the bullocks find their own way. Inevitably, the tales are told of the bullock carts that are turned around by some joker, and the peasant wakes up to find himself back where he started!

The European population of Delhi is nothing like that of Calcutta, which is home to nearly 14,000 Britons alone. Nonetheless, the diplomatic activity of Delhi is such that a large number of foreigners live there, and the parties of the diplomatic corps are popular in a state where near prohibition exists. In Bombay you must have a permit to drink; in Calcutta you must have the money to drink; in Delhi you must be a club member to drink. Indeed, in Delhi you are not supposed to have more than a certain (small) number of bottles in your home at any one time, so the alternative is the club. No drink is served in restaurants – there are, of course, no pubs – and hence the Indian businessman will always relish a trip to Calcutta where it is free to all – at a price – but on the expense account anyway. Night life in Delhi is thus restricted; there is dancing at the two or three main restaurants, the bands either imported – perhaps from the Philippines or some other strange place – or local players, many of whom are Anglo-Indians. Curiously enough, one of India's premier dance bands – Western style – if not the best one, is the Indian Navy band, who will play for quite a modest fee and for much longer than the designated hours if a drop of rum is available from time to time.

For the tourist in Delhi there is the usual array of ancient monuments – is there a country in the world which will not fall over backwards in an effort to produce some such relics of their past? In India's case, they can produce a fair collection of temples which date back a thousand years or so. These temples are of interest, and also of delight, because for some strange reason the good people of that time had an intense interest in what we might term (unkindly) pornography. They are popular places for the amateur photographer today, but in the absence of the camera in those early days they got cracking on stone, with which they constructed their places of worship. One skips a few hundred years until the Moghul period of the 17th and 18th centuries, which produced the Taj Mahal at Agra and most of the fine buildings of ancient Delhi, their one-time capital. The very important exception to this is the Qutb Minar, a column of great height erected a thousand years ago; there is also the iron pillar which refuses to rust, a result of which is that you are invited to believe that the world's most advanced metallurgists were the Indians of hundreds of years ago. These are to be seen a few miles from Delhi. The British era produced the fine government buildings of the present century. The post 1947 era brought other temples of worship to the fore, epitomised by the mighty Bhakra Nangal dam at the foot of the Himalayas.

Also whilst in Delhi you can see the Red Fort of Aurungzeb, one of the greatest of the Moghul Emperors. As a fort it is pretty useless, and has never been otherwise – it is in a position to protect nothing. Nonetheless, the main entrance looks straight down the Chandni Chowk, a wide street which Aurungzeb used for his ceremonial parades and which is now one of the liveliest, and dirtiest, of Delhi's markets. When you walk down it, take a look up at the second and third storeys of the buildings – it is amazing how they remain up there, so fragile do the structures appear. Of course, from time to time they do tumble, which explains the occasional open space reminiscent of a bombsite. Watch out for the trams, the most ancient imaginable – it is just possible to discern that they were painted yellow at some stage in their history, but the stage was not recent. You may enjoy the ride on the tram – if you can get on through the crowds, and if you do, you'll at least have the consolation of knowing that there is only a hundred to one chance that you'll be bothered for your fare. The conductor has a hopeless job, and from time to time he stops the tram, walks round it collecting a few annas to appease his employers and clambers on again. For the driver the lounging cattle are particularly difficult if they happen to have found a shady spot between the tramlines!

Perhaps you have seen enough of Chandni Chowk, its beggars – who do their rounds of the stalls, getting their regular dole from each one – the noise and the heat. You will also be shown Humayun's tomb, which is another Moghul relic, the Moghul observatory of Jantar Mantar and, best of all, the Birla Temple. This was built by one of India's richest industrialists in the 1930s and is a magnificent Hindu temple on the outskirts of New Delhi. It is cool, it is refreshing; you can take flash photographs; there are no services or sermons, although you can join the religious chanting in one of the chambers that constitute the temple; you have a fair choice of gods to worship and thus it caters for a goodly proportion of the population. All of this is yours with one stipulation – shoes off, please. If you are suspicious of the state of your

8

feet, there is a tub of water at the entrance especially for your kind.

I have mentioned Old Delhi; I have mentioned New Delhi. But Delhi itself is in fact a state, a centrally administered area, mostly on the right bank of the Jumna River, about 20 miles long and 20 wide. It contains areas known as 'New' Old Delhi, 'Old' New Delhi and 'New' New Delhi. Quite simple really, especially after a year or two of struggling with the terms. Old Delhi is that part which had its heyday up to the 1860s and, of course, is still the home of most of Delhi's lakhs (hundreds of thousands) of people; 'New' Old Delhi refers to the area built up after the 1857 troubles, which was the residential area to the north – don't ask me why there is no 'Old' Old Delhi; perhaps it would be too insulting. New Delhi is essentially the creation of this century, the seat of government, whilst 'New' New Delhi is the area which has sprung up since 1945 and which consists mainly of middle- – and upper- – class residential suburbs to the south.

Connaught Place is the shopping centre of New Delhi. It is in the form of a circle with a large park in the centre. There is plenty of parking space and here one finds whatever imported merchandise still manages to squeeze itself into the country. It would appear that dubious American paperbacks get past the customs people much more easily than baby foods. Of course, the alternative conclusion to draw is that the demand for baby foods ensures their rapid disappearance, whilst because nobody wants Western sex books, they remain above the counter unsold. There are no departmental stores in Delhi. Remember that although the population is large, purchasing power is appallingly low. Thus these shops cater mainly for the wealthy Indian and the foreigner. If you decide to wear saris in future, you cannot get a better selection than from some of the Cannaught Place stores. On the other hand, assuming you are of the opposite sex, the Khadi Emporium will present you with magnificent bush shirts, in return for which you need only part with the rupee equivalent of seven shillings.

So you have seen Delhi of the historians, of the shopper, of government. It is a capital city to be proud of, and the Indian authorities are ensuring it will remain that way by their town planning measures.

CHAPTER 2
TO AGRA

If you travel a little further south – 100 miles to be precise – you will find Agra, the home of the Taj Mahal. But in order to experience a novel form of travel, may I suggest that you select a period of the year when the roads are flooded. Having done this, you will immediately realise that your best form of transport is the motor scooter, and this is why: you reach the first of the floods; the water is a mere two or three inches deep and you proudly drive straight through. But then comes a perfectly horrible stretch, which is littered with the vehicles of the courageous who attempted to drive through it and failed. The lorry drivers are not a bit perturbed and lie snoozing on top of whatever their vehicles are carrying – with one exception. He has had the misfortune of tipping his lorry over at an alarming angle, and he and his pals are trying desperately to unload before the truck tips over completely and all his boxes slip into the water. But we, the motor scooterists, commandeer a tonga (horse and cart), at an exorbitant fee, mind you. We heave the scooter onto the footrest of the cart and clamber on after it. Praying that the footrest – designed to bear the weight of one or two featherweight peasants – does not give way, the poor half-starved horse is cajoled into the floodwater. Apart from almost losing his balance a couple of times, we slowly make the dry parts again, and with a feeling of exhilaration that inclines us to give the reversed V sign to those less fortunate, we are on our way again.

But this is getting monotonous – more floods, more expense, more hearts-in-mouth. Why not the railway line? By driving along the narrow path by the edge of the track you just can't get a foot wet – unless you topple down the bank from your razor's edge roadway. Linesmen and signalmen are courteous and helpful, informing one when the next train is due. Difficulties arise with signals, however, as they must be connected to the signal box by an annoying wire, which from time to time crosses the path. These are dealt with in the manner of one holding apart barbed wire for the girlfriend to get into the woods – by one foot pressing the wire hard against the ground as the scooter is wheeled over. The only snag is to check that you haven't switched the signal from 'danger' to 'all-clear'! You will encounter other problems – stations, for example. However, by the time an amazed stationmaster has grasped the fact that a scooter is belting up the ramp of his platform and along the full length of it, you are down the other side and on your way. In fact, if a train is standing in the station, many passengers will have missed it as they turn to gape at you. If you come to any bridges, you should be warned that they consist of the rails, the sleepers and nothing else, so the following is a recommended procedure, though not laid down in the Indian Railways handbook: put the scooter wheels on the rail and inch by inch wheel it across while jumping from sleeper to sleeper. I am assuming that you have checked whether any trains are due – if you haven't, and the worst happens, you will have to rely on personal initiative, which will probably take the form of jumping into the river and abandoning the scooter.

Thus, if you have arrived at Agra by this means, the Taj Mahal will be an anti-climax. Nevertheless, I should record that this tomb, made of marble and encrusted with diamonds, was built by Shah Jahan for his wife. The diamonds have unfortunately been removed, but certain additions have been made, for which, among other things of course, we must thank the Americans. You will espy a couple of large eye-bolts sticking from the dome, and in answer to your enquiry you must not expect to learn about some romantic quirk of the builder. They were put there as recently as 1945 so that illuminations could be festooned about in celebration of VJ day.

There is much to see at Agra and in the neighbouring Fatepur Sikri, now a dead town, which though majestic was inhabited for only a few years, as the water supply mysteriously failed. Finally, one advantage in going when there are floods about is that you will not have to fight your way through the hordes of tourists, who arrive in much greater numbers than ever saw the Changing the Guard at Buckingham Palace.

CHAPTER 3
INTO RAJASTHAN

'Do not go out after dark unless armed. Beware of tigers.' Thus reads the notice at the Maharajah's ex-palace, now a tourist hotel. We were deep in Rajasthan – that so-called land of desert, barren enough for the film North West Frontier to be shot there. But in the past it was not so barren, and the mountains around may almost have been in the Lake District in high summer, for believe it or not, water abounded. The castle, high over the lake, looked across miles of water – not to bikini-clad lasses sunbathing, but to one or two tiny villages which eked out an existence on the shores of the lake by a little cultivation and raising some buffaloes. Civilisation was apparently far away, but not in our chateau. There, the electricity was switched on at dusk, produced by a private generator.

Only four hours previously we had been in Delhi. We sped south until the road narrowed to the width of the car. It was at this point that the fun started, for either side of the tarmac was slimy mud and either you or the oncoming lorry had to get out into it. So there was a battle of nerves over who would hold the road the longer, one or the other suddenly veering off into the mud and averting disaster by about five – certainly no more than six – millimetres. Usually the lorries won. If you were lucky, you could keep the offside wheels on the tarmac, otherwise it was tricky to get back on the road. The routine is for passengers to close their eyes – the luxury of looking death in the face could be braved by only the most stalwart back-seat driver. But when one got used to it, there was at least the joy of looking at the driving mirror and seeing the effect on the lorry driver: although he had held the road, the margin was so small that reflex action on his part compelled him to turn off after we had passed. So he was in the ditch, too! Indian roads can be considered from two points of view. First, a comparison with the road networks in Western countries leads one to despair. But on the other hand, the volume of traffic using the roads is such that one can be amazed that they have bothered to provide roads at all. And kindly bear in mind that the lack of roads means that you can hardly lose yourself, for there is but the solitary road to travel along. The only danger is in going past your objective.

The flatness of Delhi gives way to rolling hills. Bends in the road take one by surprise, and the 'suburbs' give way to towns with names such as Sohna, Wuh, Fatepurjirka and, 80 miles on, Alwar, one of the great princely states of pre-independence times, where the milestones ignore that irrelevant nonentity Delhi, and instead tell you how far you are from Alwar City. It was a land of strife in 1947 when the poverty-stricken Muslims were ousted lock, stock and barrel. Many crossed the state border into the southern Punjab, but not the Meos Tribe who are a somewhat forgotten community with a reputation for lawlessness. But poor as they are, they will help the traveller on his way with advice on the state of the roads and retort with an enquiry as to why on earth you want to go that way. The capital, Alwar, is a well laid out town, although the concentration of humans in the bazaar area makes the rest of the well-conceived town irrelevant, if not irreverent. The Maharajah's palace is some miles out and, like most, in a beautiful situation. Here, too, is a lake of some grandeur and the terraces echo a life of elegance and grace, which has now faded. The cabinet room is full of relics of the past – the photographs of historic meetings, the chairs and thrones which were used, pictures of the great Alwar army, an army which fought in North Africa in two world wars. Today, however, the Alwar family are noted for shikar (hunting) and for a wonderful collection of ancient motorcars, which were not collected on shikar. The Maharajah's powers are now reduced to nothing, although his personal reputation is such that he is still a respected person in his state.

We are not concerned with this gentleman but with another of his palaces, the Palace of Silliserh, which the Government of Rajasthan regard as a tourist attraction. What a joy it is, arriving hot and tired, to sink into the fabulously thick carpets and open some cold beer. The contrast with the hot and sticky journey is incredible and in that lies the satisfaction:

the savouring of the cool breeze which wafts across the lake through the open doors and windows. A sleep is definitely called for after lunch and to awake for a wash and tea at about four o'clock. Then the day can recommence with a trip on the lake, a swim or a walk – but be back before dark! In the perfect silence of the evening, on the balcony overlooking the lake, the moon provides all the light necessary in which to talk and to drink. Suddenly, in the distance, a roar. Yes, although the Maharajah cut down most of the trees in his domain during his tiger hunts, there are tigers still to be found. From time to time, the tourist manager is confronted with one. But in this day and age he carries no gun with which he can dispose of the tiger. If he had a truck he might run it over and get away with it, but no, he rides a scooter. The routine is to stop (I should emphasise that this course of action is not yet widely accepted), switch off the headlight, for the ray of light attracts the tiger, and then rev the scooter up to an almighty din, thus scaring the animal off. If this fails with any of my readers, please accept my apologies.

The next day, averaging 30 miles an hour, we reached Jaipur in three hours. What a drive. Through forest-clad hills, through well-cultivated valleys, over mountains as desolate as those of northern Scotland, to arrive at one of India's great tourist centres. If you are familiar with New York, then you will know of the street planning – the streets running parallel to each other and the avenues cutting across at right angles. Indians, however, have not got to go so far afield for their examples; only to Jaipur, planned and built hundreds of years ago with its wide streets – the sewers in the centre of the roads but recently covered over. It is a charming town and if one could afford one of the beautiful houses in the suburbs one could indeed be in heaven with the one proviso – air conditioning!

But it is five miles from Jaipur that the main interest lies: the old capital of Amber set strategically in the pass, which invaders and travellers must use to get to Jaipur. From here, the old walls stretch on either side, up and down the mountainsides, reminiscent of pictures of the Great Wall of China. The well-preserved ruin – 300 years old – is still little affected by the ravages of time in this land, which does not have to battle against the rain, snow and smog from which our own buildings suffer so severely. And so you can still see the bathing pool on the roof, which could still be used today but for the difficulty of getting the scores of men needed to carry the water up to it – although pulling the plug out is still no difficulty. In this old relic of a time not so long past it is likely that the guide will extol the synthesis of cultures which has gone into constructing the building. It is a theme which Indians are very keen about and they will tell you of the basic Hindu culture, organisation and architecture which existed and which were adopted by the Muslim invaders from the north hundreds of years ago. In this part of India the invaders arrived late, and whilst the rulers adopted certain aspects of Mohammedan culture, they were not engulfed until later – it is thus in the region closer to Delhi and the northern plains that one finds the great relics of Moghul rule – the Red Fort at Delhi and that most famous of all monuments, the Taj Mahal.

However, as like as not, your guide will be a beautiful girl from the tourist office – which is bad policy really, for one will find a much more charming synthesis of cultures to attend to and one's history of India suffers accordingly. You will understand that the Indian Tourist Office is using the same gimmick that progressive organisations in this country use. You will find that these girls can put over a great deal of information – in many respects the educated women of India have their feet much more on the ground than their menfolk.

Back to Jaipur and we are on the road south. The Rajasthani women are frequently very colourful – looking from the feet up, if I may, bangles on ankles (nothing on the feet), flared skirt, bra (bare midriff) and cloak, which is really headgear, for it billows open revealing the top half of the lady, which boasts only the bikini-like bra.

The stretch of road from Jaipur to Ajmer, 80 miles to the south, has a magnificent surface, although it is only wide enough for one car. Being virtually dead straight, high speeds are possible in between the herds of goats, but then one's average speed is dragged down precipitously by the time taken to honk them off the road. The drover is frequently indignant that a car should interpose itself on a road which is virtually the monopoly of him and his goats. This is not surprising, for during the whole of the 80-mile stretch I saw only half a dozen other vehicles. At the end of the road – almost literally so, for after Ajmer there is little but desert stretching away to Pakistan – is the fine old town which appears as a true desert city from the Circuit House atop the hill by the lake. It is the lake which gives Ajmer its charm and without it, it would not exist.

For anybody who has not seen an Eastern 'laundry' at work, there is no better place than from this Circuit House. Below, in the shallows, dozens of dhobis are about their task and the still air carries their grunts as they strain at their work. The procedure is simple, although it more closely resembles the mime of a road worker with a pickaxe. Your best shirt, plus one or two belonging to others, is swung back over the shoulder and then swung over again and beaten against a rock with a resounding whack. Strangely, neither shirt nor stone split and the procedure is continued until no dirt has the audacity to remain attached to the shirt. As no soap is used, no rinsing process is necessary and the launderette's spin driers are replaced by a strong sun. However, in the monsoon season it is often difficult to dry the clothes properly in the open and on such occasions you will notice a peculiar odour as you clamber into your clean shirt. If you cannot identify it, I should tell you that it is the aroma of smoke from a cow dung-fuelled fire.

You cannot get far from people in India. In this semi-desert area, where only poor steppe and scrub exist, you will come across the women-folk looking for bits of shrubbery worth burning for their fires, and a camel may be tagging along looking for something to eat. Herds of goats apparently survive on this poor diet, which must surely consist of 75% sand. Yet even the most barren of India's land must produce something for these peasants, and it is clear that these Rajasthanis have every incentive to depart for Delhi to earn £3 per month on the building sites.

The Automobile Association told me quite definitely that the road was open and free from floodwater. It was no use my telling them that a fellow traveller had attempted it the previous day and had had to turn back. They had been informed by the Executive Engineer, Public Works Department of the district that the road was clear, so passable it must be. I wonder how many other poor fools tried and failed on that road. Instead of asking for a refund of my subscription, I ignored their 'advice' and planned myself a detour. An alternative route, 200-odd miles longer, had, in addition to the direct route out of Rajasthan, been flooded by the worst monsoon in history three months previously, but cars were getting through. So this road I took and found that by travelling across a track worn by previous traffic through fields, I could detour the worst of the floods.

But I was to regret the decision. A huge area perhaps 30 miles by 20 miles was virtually under water and it was obviously necessary to drain it into the rivers. In order to facilitate this exercise, the ingenious idea was devised of hacking away the roadway – which was built on an embankment a few feet above the surrounding fields – to let the water out. This had certainly proved a success and the water was flowing through the breach. Like all good things, it had its difficult side – in the form of how to get a car across! As luck would have it, the Indian army were on manoeuvres that day – not an amphibious exercise; that came later. The captain in the jeep swore I could get across, as the water was not as high as my exhaust. Fair enough, so away I went. All went well until the car hit a patch of stones in which the wheels revolved desperately, thereby digging themselves deeper into a better resting place. A few more moments and the exhaust was submerged and the engine gave up. Slowly, the water slopped into the car – boot and all – and I was desperate.

The kindly army captain in the jeep felt a twinge of guilt, and playing on this I persuaded him to acquire a rope and haul me out. Half an hour later it arrived and the operation started, but the car would not be moved and the only result was a broken rope. The feeling of desperation grew, which was not helped by the arrival of a bus and its load of passengers. It was made clear to me what I should not have done when the bus driver pointed out that he could not get his bus across until my car was got out of the way –

either onto the road or pushed into deeper water! Once again, three cheers for the Indian army – and the bus passengers – who were joyfully induced to take off shoes and socks (those who boasted them) and roll up their pants. While the jeep pulled desperately, a dozen kindly souls, roaring with laughter at my plight, lifted the car. Suddenly, with a lurch forward, we were on dry land. Nobody would take an anna – they had all had a good morning and I was left to the job of mopping out the car and hoping that the differential, engine and a dozen other parts were still in working order.

And so out of Rajasthan, one of the most colourful of India's states, where the women's bright red costumes belie the poverty of the land. It is the land of the Rajputs and the warrior races, a land of magnificent palaces and wonderful scenery. Only in the west of the state is the land a parched desert. But before we leave, let us take a trip to Seriska Palace, now open to the tourist, in the depths of shikar country. You will be invited to stay and board at £1 per day; optional 'extras' include an item which you will not get even in the best hotels in Park Lane. Should you wish to take photographs of a tiger, then part with another pound and a kid goat or baby calf will be yours. At least you do not have to take personal possession of it, but it will be strung up – alive, I am afraid – and a tiger, getting its scent, will approach it cautiously and 'see it off'. In this way, if you have not been shivering with fear too much or merely fainting, you will have one or two interesting photographs for the folks back home.

If this is too expensive, too bloodthirsty or too nerve-racking, there is another unlisted amenity. Tip a couple of bearers to drag out one of the many stuffed tigers or panthers from its showcase and have it parked in a strategic spot in the grounds. This arranged, invite your friends for a walk and you, being very callous, will enjoy their reactions when they meet your friend, the dummy ...

CHAPTER 4
THE PUNJAB

Chandigarh is the capital of India's Punjab state. Formerly, Lahore – now in Pakistan – was the chief town of the pre-1947 undivided Punjab. So a new capital was needed, but where to site it? They could have moved to Amritsar, but that was considered to be dangerously near the border; the underdeveloped south of the state was considered miles from anywhere – except Delhi, which is a state on its own. The one existing alternative was Jullundur, a thriving town and commercial centre of the Punjab. Instead, the Punjabis chose a brand new spot; it lay at the foot of the mighty Himalayas, which provide a magnificent backdrop to the town; it is just about as far away from Pakistan as you can get in India's Punjab, and it gave the planners free rein for their conceptions of the future and futuristic India.

To plan the place, Le Corbusier was called in, all the way from France, and he proceeded to devise a town which can only be described as the Brasilia of India. A little less great in conception, but on the same lines with its modernistic architecturally diverse buildings, only having the futuristic theme in common. The layout of the town is well defined, but what a place to find one's way about! Try and find Sector 24, Street 8, and No. 14, and you've got a job and a half on your hands. It's fine if you happen to find yourself moving along Sector 20 upwards in your search, but if at 23 you came to the edge of the town, do you turn left, right, or is 24 at the base of the ladder once again? Give me the complicated London street plan, which is patently impossible, rather than the apparent simplicity of Chandigarh!

Each area is laid out as residential, shopping, light industry, government, schools and so on. The residential area is again split up by social levels, or rather economic strata of society. The best housing is naturally that of ministers of government and high officials, and whilst good it is by no means elaborate. It is interesting that the layout of homes resembles the pattern in Britain: three bedrooms, two reception rooms, kitchen and two bathrooms. It is remarkable that a Punjab minister's home is no more lavish than that of a modest detached home with garage and garden in Britain. And what is more, he is not entitled to air conditioning. Only fans rotate to keep him and his family cool, although air conditioning is built into some of the more important public buildings.

As with most new towns, either in Britain or in India, Chandigarh has no life or character. It is deemed to be an intellectual backwater, but it is very much to the future that such towns look. Chandigarh is far from complete, for financially it is an incredibly heavy burden for an Indian state to shoulder, and it is inevitable that its construction will be spread out over many years. So ten years hence add this new town to your list of tourist attractions, for there you will be able to relax in air-conditioned hotels and sail and swim in the huge artificial lake now under construction.

In frightening contrast is Ludhiana, a town of about 250,000 souls, about 50 miles away to the west and south of Chandigarh. It is, I fear, the prototype of industrial India, a product of excessively free enterprise and a foretaste of many Indian cities to come, for it is on the products of such centres that India will prosper. On the foundation of squalor and cheap-jack workshops and factories, industrial India will grow as Britain grew in the years of the Industrial Revolution. Here we find private enterprise – the enterprise mainly of Sikhs – making bicycles, nuts and bolts, textiles, and in the course of it, preparing the people for their future heritage. There is no doubt of the town's prosperity – on the outskirts one encounters many brick kilns, which in their own small way are symbolic of progress and relative prosperity. Then one sees the new government institutions, colleges of agriculture, of research into this and that, and the cinemas. You can use the number of cinemas quite happily as the criterion of prosperity of any Indian provincial town. They are themselves the most palatial of buildings – relative to Indian standards – brilliantly lit at night, and their pseudo-luxury is in stark contrast to their drab surroundings. Ludhiana has half a dozen.

The factories and workshops are erected anywhere without civic direction or aesthetic considerations; thus the most fantastic array of 'buildings' appears. In a single street one will find a scruffy yard with a brick-built hut boasting a splash of corrugated iron on the top. Inside will be the sweating workers, using the light which comes from the exposed fourth side of the structure. Next to it will be a reasonably pukka building, proudly boasting real glass windows, with the owner's bungalow alongside. Next to it, a tented school with the children attempting to study above the din of the workshop. It is difficult to describe the absence of tidiness; the place displays all aspects of the lives of the workers, and the food shop and teashop, constructed of jute bags and poles and little else, make their appearance and add their element of dilapidation to the scene.

But let us move on to Ferozpur, a border town on the road to nowhere. It has all the charm of an old-walled city, with its colourful bazaar and the old buildings which give an indication of the lost prosperity of the place. It has the virtue that its inevitable dilapidation is not heightened by industrial dirt – one can find it in one's heart to excuse the depredations of age. There is no industry in the town except that of catering for the army. It is an important cantonment town, being so close to the Pakistan frontier. A visit to the cantonment club recalls British days – understandably, for it was built in 1849, just three years after the end of the Sikh wars, which brought this region under British rule. Yet today its lofty ballroom, its bars, bridge and billiards rooms are still used, and the place has not yet the deserted and uncared-for look of so many such places one encounters across India today. Indeed, in the cantonment, with its peaceful tree-shaded roads, one has difficulty in locating any barracks or military installations. But on the outskirts you will come across some Nissen huts – Nissen huts in India's heat: I don't envy the sepoys (private soldiers) their accommodation, but I do hope that they never store ammunition in them. These cantonment areas are not under the control of the local civic authorities, but of the Military Cantonment Boards, who conduct all the functions of the civilian authority. In fact, the state of the roads, amenities, drainage and town planning in general are invariably superior to those of the adjacent town. They are policed by the military and not by the civil or state police. Their reputation, throughout India, is such that the middle and upper class Indian, being transferred to another town, will try his damnedest to get a house in the cantonment. It is possible to do so in some towns not close to strategic areas such as Bareilly in Uttar Pradesh, whose cantonment is now of little military significance.

A mile or two out of the town is the bridge across the Sutlej River – it is quiet now, for no trains have crossed it for many years and the road bridge seldom carries a car. In fact, few cross the river at all, except armed police going to and from the Indian border post, which is, for some strange reason, situated on the west side of the river. The occasional fishing craft has in recent years been joined by another species of craft belonging to the armies of both India and Pakistan, which cruise up and down this area, watching out for intruders from either side.

From Ferozpur you travel to Amritsar. The area through which you move has consolingly been described as one of the most lawless in India. For those of you who have been indoctrinated about the dacoits (thieves) of the area south of Delhi, this is not the sort of tourist attraction you want to hear about. However, if you give your storyteller time, he will mention that harvest time is the most dangerous but that the gentlemen of the region are not interested in you, the occasional intruder. Instead, they are concerned with the many feuds which seem to sprout in the healthy Punjab climate, and they choose the harvest period to do their bumping-off so that the sale of their crops will enable them to employ a good lawyer to defend them in court!

The Sikh population of Amritsar do not appear to notice that they are living 15 miles from Pakistan – and why should they? Life is very placid here, and proof of their confidence in the future is to be seen in the ribbon development – in the best Great West Road tradition – which stretches along the road through Cheharta towards the border post at Attari. The only thing they appear to deplore is the inability to go into Lahore for a boozy night out. Amritsar was, and is, extremely prosperous – it is perhaps the most prosperous provincial city in India – and the Sikhs will leave you in no doubt as to why it is so prosperous, and why they call it the Birmingham of the Punjab. Although virtually no Muslims were left after partition, many poverty-stricken Kashmiri Muslims are now coming into Amritsar to share in the general prosperity. This they do by displacing horses – or rather oxen – and you see them pushing coal-carts and other merchandise around. Their labour is presumably more economic than the employment of motor vehicles or beasts of burden.

The heart of the city – the bazaar area – is reminiscent of the blitzed areas of London. From time to time one comes across devastated areas, which, one is told, were the sites of Muslim homes and mosques – none now exist in Amritsar. But Amritsar is famous also for another massacre – that of 1919, when General Dwyer fired on a large assembly at Jallianawalla Park, which had collected in defiance of an edict against the holding of meetings. He killed 2,000 and today the Park is in the process of preservation as a national shrine, where even the bullet marks on the walls are preserved and marked. Also preserved for posterity is the well in which so many died when they threw themselves into it in the attempt to avoid the hail of bullets. But Amritsar is to the Sikh what the Vatican is to the Roman Catholic. Here is their Golden Temple set in an artificial lake which is emptied once a year for cleaning – and it is considered an honour to help in this work. The temple itself is small, rather disappointingly small, but partially covered in gold leaf, which is an anti-climax to the naive tourist who envisaged it as one great mass of solid gold.

Jullundur is the commercial capital of the Punjab, still very annoyed that it was not chosen as the seat of government. Its civic pride was severely shaken when a stretch of agricultural land was selected in preference to the enchantments of the scruffy town. Most of the Punjab's newspapers emanate from the byways of Jullundur, written not only in Hindi, but in Punjabi and Urdu also. A word in your ear – these newspapers are not the mammoths of the West, which have daily circulations counted in millions and correspondents in every part of the globe. Mind you, they do have their correspondents, but on further investigation one will find that the bloke who styles himself as the correspondent in Britain is probably a Sikh working on British Railways at Camden Town. From this vantage point, sixpenny airmail letters are addressed to his editor in Jullundur, and the facts of British life are circulated in the Punjab to all of the paper's 5,000 readers. You will kindly note that the Punjabi script is so large that it requires three times the number of pages for a similar quantity of verbiage in English. Moreover, these good souls who are hampered by having to produce Urdu publications cannot rely on the use of typewriters, for none is available so far for their complicated script, which resembles, but is not identical to, Arabic. They have the extra disadvantage of having to start at the right-hand side of the page and work over to the left. They do it sitting on cushions, leaning back against the wall of the newspaper office, to produce some of the most beautiful handwriting – so I am told by experts in the language. Those people who eulogise the virtues of the Urdu script are no doubt in the same category as those people in this country who deplore the departure of copperplate writing.

It must be that every paper in the Punjab has flogged to death the wonders of Britain, the welfare state and so on, for in Jullundur are to be found a profusion of travel agencies. There are probably more travel agencies in the main street than there are pubs in the main street of an English naval port. To find where they acquire their business is no less startling – from the good peasant who mortgages his land to buy his ticket and, frequently, his forged passport, and then away he goes to the promised land, which for some strange reason, as often as not, is Coventry. Prosperity in the surrounding villages is in no small measure due to remittances from overseas.

Near Jullundur is found one of the most developed villages in the country – Khajurla. In this village, cottage industries are successful; khadi (shirt cloth) is made and sold, soap is made and simple sewing is taught to the girls, who use their talents to make clothes for their dowry. Co-operative effort has eliminated unemployment, and the Public Works Department gives roadwork to gangs of villagers. However, contractors do not favour this and considerable strife does occur when the contractors attempt to bribe the PWD. Even latrines of brick are being built, with soakaway pits underneath. They are used and then the site is changed, but not all the villagers avail themselves of these newfangled facilities. Manure pits have proved quite successful for the creation of fertiliser, while artificial fertiliser is also obtained through the Co-operative Bank. Although the population of the village is only 3,000, the credit balance to the village at the bank has reached Rs. 70,000 (£5,000). This is an incredible sum for an Indian village to have accumulated. All the lanes have been bricked (never paved) and immaculate cleanliness is apparent everywhere. I was told by the Community Development Officer that the response to proposals for improvements is good and easy to obtain, provided the approach is tactful. In Khajurla the panchayat (council) is a good one, and the headman (sarpanch) was once an NCO in the army. This enlightened gentleman, and his effective panchayat, levies taxes on cycles and chulas (stoves), and imposes fines for lack of window spaces for ventilation in houses and for illegal distillation of the local hooch.

This area of the Northern Punjab is the land of the Punjabi Suba, the hoped for Sikh state, where the Sikh majority areas have been designated and the Punjabi language – not Hindi – is the medium of instruction in the schools. Hindu and Sikh work quite amiably together, so don't be deceived by those wearing the Muslim fur cap, for they are merely wearing it to protect themselves in the winter's cold. In the confused struggle for and against the further division of the Punjab between Sikhs and Hindus, the story is told of a group of Hindus who were arrested for rioting in favour of the Hindi language and required to sign their names in Hindi. They were unable to do so – instead they used Punjabi, the language of their opponents, the Sikhs.

The monsoon produces a crop without much bother: wheat, maize and cotton; and sugar cane, which takes the best part of the year to grow. But the bright sunshine of winter will only produce a crop if irrigation facilities are there to provide the water to nourish the soil. The snow of the Himalayas produces the water – it merely requires man to store it until required and direct it to the land which needs it. In this modern age, ingenious man has thought of producing electricity and fishing grounds as sidelines, and at virtually no extra cost.

It was more than 50 years ago that they first started digging the canals that would bring water to the desert and the one-crop-a-year land. The mighty network of canals, built at a time when nobody had a thought to spare for Pakistan, was until recently a source of dispute between the two countries as to who should have the water from where. But disregarding the politics in the picture, the canals have continued to function over the past 40 or more years. During this time the seepage from those unlined canals (they are merely excavations and are not lined by bricks to prevent seepage) has understandably been enormous. A stage has now been reached where the adjacent areas are on the point of being waterlogged – waterlogged to the extent that land is beginning to go out of cultivation. In the Punjab, on both sides of the frontier, it is becoming a serious problem and experts declare that the water table is now a mere one to six feet below the fields.

Many solutions have been suggested, particularly that of lining the canals, but this would be a stupendous undertaking. A foreign expert has suggested the most obvious solution (and perhaps the most naive): to take the water away in water carts and dump it in the river. Land drainage by piping, as in England, is also too expensive. In practice, the farmer has his own solution – he digs a ditch and drains the water off his land, and then the next bloke has the job of getting rid of it – and so on. This, of course, does not happen without generating what we might call a little tension between villagers. It is envisaged, however, that the new Bhakra Canal and the new Rajasthan Canal, both taking water from the Sutlej River, will largely replace the existing network and relieve the problem of waterlogging by feeding the desert area of Rajasthan with the badly needed elixir of life. The incredible ramifications of this Bhakra scheme will also mean that the waters of the Jumna River will be able to serve more of Uttar Pradesh – on the left back of the river – rather than supplying parts of the Punjab as at present.

There is, of course, a limit to the purposes that you can adapt a multi-purpose project for, and these canals, leading from mountains to desert, are hardly likely to prove useful in transportation. So please take warning and do not comment, as did the diplomat who had spent his war service near the Suez Canal, "Disgraceful, all those wonderful canals being wasted – not a ship on them!"

Is there any cricketer who has not heard the name of the Nawab of Pataudi? Yes! Well, I apologise, for I know little of his cricket career, except that he was a renowned cricketer and that the present Nawab is following in his footsteps. But he was not only a cricketer. Eighteen miles south of Delhi, and still in the Punjab, is the municipality of Gurgaon, a town of some 20,000 souls. I should hate you to imagine a metropolis – in India 20,000 people are easily crammed into a square mile and it is not necessary to provide multi-storey flats to do so. Only recently has the luxury of a suburb tentatively revealed itself in Gurgaon. But having honked one's way through the bazaar, and during the trip acquired a few more scrapes on the car's paintwork, a narrow, almost non-existent road displays a signpost to Pataudi. So away one goes, finding the roadway by a process of elimination – where the least sand rests. Mine is probably the first car during the week, and it is Saturday. Between the sand dunes one slithers along like a modern Moses between the bulrushes. The tarmac is in need of repair – if I'm not careful the sharp edges will play havoc with the car's tyres. All good things come to an end, and even the unsavoury roadway dwindles almost to nothing and forgets its tarmac. But then we are at the entrance, or the exit, to the town of Pataudi. Granted there are no forbidding notices for pushbikes, invalid chairs and other hazards, but we are told by a monument that the strip of nature just traversed was opened as a road in pre-war days by the Nawab, thus linking him with Delhi and with visiting cricket teams.

Heat, toil and thirst compelled a halt at one of the local chain of self-service restaurants. This involved edging a camel and its cart a little further along and squeezing in beside a sand dune and the recently constructed 'restaurant'. It is unlikely that a similar structure would figure in the London plan, but town planning in Pataudi is in its infancy. The tea served was good and the cups clean. This was inspired by my request to pour boiling water over them as an inducement to keep the flies at bay.

One of the main problems of the tourist in the state of Pataudi is to be sure that he is devoting his attention to the state and not to the Punjab. This is because the state is just about sufficiently large to incorporate a cricket pitch and little else! A guide can be obtained by request from the Kutchery, or Whitehall of Pataudi, to be found inside the state's fort. The palace of the Nawab is reminiscent of a large English country house. It is of modest size – compared to an English country house, not in relation to the size of Pataudi. As one might expect, the front garden is a cricket pitch – never used now – and inside are pictures of the Nawab playing cricket. Moreover, the largest carpet I have seen in my life is spread across the main banqueting hall. It must be about 100 feet by 40. The bathrooms are magnificent, but no running water is available to supply the taps. Our guide showed us round the flat-topped roof from where one could see the full extent of the state – all two square miles of it. My guide was also at pains to show the photographs of the Pataudi State Guard – the English equivalent is to be seen any day outside Buckingham Palace.

The guide, with a beard any Muslim could be proud of, was most diligent (Pataudi is a Muslim Empire surrounded by the Sikhs and Hindus of the Punjab). But the guide would not accept my profferred tip. After he had departed I found out the reason for the refusal by the old gentleman – he was the erstwhile Attorney General of the State of Pataudi ... and so once again, no doubt, the topic of conversation in that tiny state of north India was the condescension and arrogance of the British.

In two short minutes we were back in the Punjab and to the rest house at Tauru. What a charming place! A place of beauty, serenity, peace and – natural life. Maybe there were rats in the roof, snakes in the ceiling, but to outward appearances it was ideal. The rest house was erected for the people who inspected the roads – the Public Works Department – in British days. I really take my hat off to these visiting officials; there may be an absence of roads in the area, but that was no reason for not building a rest house in a spot where such good shooting was to be had. I regret that I cannot recount from departmental files the sound reasons given before the decision to build was taken – I am only grateful that it was taken. Hence it was that I bounced the car along a dirt bank to the rest house, which is surrounded by trees and a pleasant garden. The sun's rays had departed, but in north India after March that does not mean it gets chilly. It is still very warm, and so the chowkidar (watchman) brought out chairs and a table while we listened to the sounds of Indian life over a 'cuppa' – or perhaps, if my memory suggests correctly, it was a 'glassa'.

You may wonder what there is to hear at night apart from the buses, the rows of the people next door and the rain pattering on the window between the TV programmes. But here in the heart of India it sounded like a multitude of crickets, their noise made all the more fulsome by the silence of the night. Still warm as the moon rose, the animal world had left a few human stalwarts behind in the nearby village. You do not get far from human beings in India and, through a stillness that seems almost to shatter the eardrums, the voices of the villagers from the distant 'boozer' can be heard. And so to bed – not indoors, but outside, please. You will find that a light dew comes up at about 5 a.m., but just move your featherweight bed into the verandah and sleep until daylight.

Still in the Punjab, but to the south of Delhi, it is poor land, much of it too high to be irrigated, and so the rains bring one crop a year, and sugar cane, the main cash crop, is not so frequently seen. The population is poor and none too happy about the centre of government being more than 200 miles to the north in Chandigarh. Complaints may be voiced about the roads, which are poor, and that Community Development has not come to their region. When one enquires why this should be, the people will mention the fact that they are Muslims – the Meos tribe (it was, incidentally, from this tribe that Gandhi's assassin came). They are an aggressive lot and in 1947 they were chucked out, lock, stock and barrel, from the state of Alwar and moved into the southern parts of the Punjab. Desperately poor, they claim that they are ignored by the Sikh and Hindu rulers of the state at Chandigarh and that they are regarded as a liability in an otherwise progressive state. When they raise their voices they are asked why they don't clear off to Pakistan!

There are many facets to the Punjab. But its 16 millions live in one of the better-off states of the Indian Union, and it is likely that the enterprise of its inhabitants, allied to political considerations, will keep it that way.

Not quite to motorway standards. Punjab.

Crossing the Jumna River.

Awaiting breakdown assistance. Punjab.

A Nepalese traffic jam.

V.I.P. village transport. Uttar Pradesh.

Hill porter. Himachal Pradesh.

CHAPTER 5

CALCUTTA MAIL

You have to be very poor not to use a porter. Travellers arrive by chauffeur-driven car, others by tonga and others walk. But at the station precincts it is virtually a tradition to shed your baggage, which will be taken by one of the dozens of red-shirted dhoti-clad gents awaiting your arrival. Of suitcases there are few – there are infinitely more 'bedrolls' – but regardless of size, shape or weight, they all go on the coolie's head. And if he can't put them all up there himself, then his mate will always assist. The final load scarcely allows for leeway under the highest bridge. But one free hand is devoted to carrying the odd baby, or merely for catching hold of the dhoti to wipe his nose with.

As at all railway stations, tickets must be checked before you proceed to your platform. Now many of you good people, who are used to the traditional method of some European land, which will be nameless, of ignoring footbridges, will assume that their superfluity does not need to be emphasised under Indian conditions. This is not so: footbridges will be used in acknowledgement of the signs in Hindi – and in English for the benefit of reluctant foreigners. Indeed, the Indian Railways are an organisation of considerable efficiency. Accidents are few, despite the practices described below. Stations and track are soundly constructed and lines usually above flood levels, thereby serving the purpose of a highway – for pedestrians – for the multitudes deprived of roads in the monsoon season. The occasional accident is due to the devilry of those who enjoy taking up a stretch of track occasionally and then doing a spot of plundering in the confusion of the smash-up.

The train comes in – slowly, for dozens are already jumping off and others jumping in, having flung their bedrolls in the open windows first, a hazard which should be included in the conditions of issue of the traveller's ticket. I head for a first-class, non air-conditioned coach, as I am paying my own fare and air-conditioned travel is twice as expensive. In any compartment which houses six during the day, but three at night in bunks, I expect to form part of a tiny community for 24 hours, which is the time taken to do the 1,000 miles between Delhi and Calcutta. I recollect my previous long-distance journey and my first in India – the 24-hour journey from Bombay to Delhi, having been severely warned not to drink the water, not to eat from the restaurant car and a dozen other cautions. I had arrived in Delhi not only exhausted from hunger and almost dehydrated from thirst, but with a raging cold from the icebox refrigeration known as air conditioning.

The train starts slowly, for only when it starts do people take the Anglo-Indian guard's whistle seriously, and then one sees the phenomenon otherwise unknown in India – people running to jump aboard as the train very slowly leaves the platform. It follows, as my brighter readers will have already deduced, that the British tradition of ensuring all doors are closed before starting is dispensed with. Indeed, the only attempt ever made in this direction in India met with tragedy. In Calcutta, the new electric trains were to make their inaugural run: they were resplendent with automatic doors and fast acceleration. But in traditional manner, the latecomers almost exceeded those already behind the closed doors as the train moved off. Hanging on to the handrails, the latecomers endeavoured, in vain, to open the doors, and as the train accelerated so rapidly it was impossible to jump off. As the train approached its first bridge, the arch swept them off like flies and many died. Now Calcutta's suburban electric trains run with the doors open and crawl out of stations like their predecessors.

To adjust oneself to a 24-hour railway journey is a work of art. One has not the freedom of shipboard travel to move about in this corridor-less box, nor has one the ability to stretch one's legs when tired of driving the car. So relaxation is the watchword, and I was intrigued by my fellow travellers' activities to this end. One was an army captain granted first-class travel at second-class rates. He disappeared, resplendent in uniform, beard and all, into the tiny toilet compartment, which contains a shower and WC – Eastern type. He emerged in a bush shirt and a pair of cotton trousers, which can be described as a cross between a sailor's bellbottoms and pyjama pants. On his feet was a pair of chappals – a leather sole with a thong across the toe to keep them on. This, however, was a very temporary arrangement, for when he sat down his feet were tucked up – not quite under him but to one side – in what appeared to be a most relaxed and cool position. That was only the beginning.

We hear the naive, smooth-shaved Englishman long for a beard 'to avoid shaving early in the morning'. I have never since that day yearned to be relieved of the chore of shaving. What my friend the Sikh had to do with his growth was incredible. Mind you, he had not cut his hair, or had it cut, since the day he was born – at least, that is the theory, but vanity and civilisation go together, I suppose, and adjustments are made where necessary. And so this gentleman's turban came off to reveal a glorious topknot of hair – like a woman's bun, but right on top and secured by a tiny comb. I should add another elementary detail, which will suggest my fellow-traveller's degree of sophistication: the traditional turban is a strip of cloth five yards long, but while your wife can stand at the other end of the garden holding one end, the process of tying is otherwise a little difficult. Thus the turban is frequently so starched that it can be put on and taken off like a hat.

Having undone the topknot, the flood of hair was tremendous, and it flowed about his head like a beatnik's – or a sadhu's. The effect, if not frightening, is certainly not glamorous (I am told that Sikhs make love wearing their turbans). This mass of hair was combed and replaced in the topknot, and it is at this stage that one expects to be asked whether you mind if he does not put his turban back on. Instead, silence prevails and I am fighting gallantly against the prospect of permanent cross-eyes, for all the while I am ostensibly and avidly reading a book, yet devoting my entire gaze to the spectacle. But there was more to come: the beard had to be titivated. This involved combing, cutting little snippets off moustache and ends, powdering and finally, of course, applying hair cream. Then, in order to keep the beard trim, a piece of cloth, which I can only describe as a bandage, was tied under the chin and over the head. The result of this was to give the appearance of a sorely wounded man and I almost instinctively looked for the red tie underneath. The skill involved in this is worthy of note, for the train was rocking on its way all the time.

By way of contrast, the Bengali was already in his loose dhoti – a garment best described as a muslin shirt, wrapped in an apparently haphazard manner about the lower regions, serving as a handkerchief and displaying the ungainly calves of man. This gentleman, whom one presumed was a wealthy businessman, was already at ease, feet up and picking them happily.

We were not yet on speaking terms, although I knew that the army captain would speak perfect English with ease and that the Bengali would know some. In any event, translations would be undertaken by the Sikh into Hindi, which most Bengalis can follow very well. From the obvious comfort of my companions, I was slowly becoming aware of my own discomfort. In collar and tie I was desperately hot, and shoes and socks did not add to my comfort. I thought of wearing my pyjama trousers, but the earliness of the hour deterred me, along with the open fly, which, as you may know, is a feature of Western attire. I compromised: washing my feet, I dispensed with anything on them and took off the tie.

My interest continued to follow the line of personal comfort and I began to consider the open doors – but to close them would make the heat unbearable. It was better to take a chance on falling out and to suffer the smuts from the engine and the dust from the land we passed through, which even the monsoon rains could not keep on the ground. Fortunately, it was easy to wash frequently and at every station a cup of tea was forthcoming – and later just water. In sheer desperation I put aside all qualms about the possible after effects in the form of dysentery.

I am getting used to my Bengali friend; his nasal activity is not dealt with by the dhoti – nor, of course, by a handkerchief – but instead the proceeds are propelled with magnificent accuracy by two fingers out of the window to be blown heaven knows where by the train's rush of air. And the picking of the feet, I have tried to persuade myself, is no worse than the nervous nail biting in an English train.

And so my thoughts are led to the world outside my travelling home. The sun is up and the heat is growing, and so far I have not had a moment to survey the countryside. The land we are passing through is Uttar Pradesh, the most populous state of India, having many more millions than the British Isles and mostly in villages, which the train passes every few minutes. These settlements are seldom more than a mile or two from the next and each will shelter from 500 to 10,000 souls, with the average being about 4,000. Yet all must gain their living from the soil around their village. But it is the monsoon season, the temperature is about 95°F and the relative humidity is nearing 90%. The land is flooded; wherever the train goes there are more floods and where there is no actual flooding, there is waterlogged land. Villages still emerge miraculously from the water, perched as they are five or ten feet above the surrounding level on the remnants of many previous mud villages, which were their predecessors. The walls of the mud huts are straining against the lapping waters. The populace are confined to the villages and devote themselves to their milk-giving buffalo. The buffalo love the water and the monsoon paradise allows them to stay in water as long as they wish. Indeed, it is an ill wind that blows nobody any good, and so it proves with the monsoon waters, for the milk yields of the buffalo soar enormously in the monsoon season to provide an alternative source of income for the villagers.

More floods – all the dhobis (washer men) are in their element. It is washing day with a vengeance and it is immaterial that the floodwaters are laden with mud and silt. The real problem is finding somewhere for the washing to dry, and it is not surprising that the railway embankments are used, providing a colourful fringe to the watery scene. The whole of Eastern Uttar Pradesh must be waterlogged. On first sight, the fields appear normal, but as the train passes at right angles to the furrows I can see the water lying in the trenches. The growing crops, sugar cane and maize, conceal the soaked ground below, which will remain that way until the mighty rivers – mainly the Jumna and Ganges – can drain away the surplus from the precariously high water table of the north Indian plains. And so we chug along through a very wet countryside where the only item of stability is the railway line and where the occasional road is breached so many times by floodwaters that travel along it is impossible. A week or so later I travelled by air over this landscape and it was clear that almost the whole area was, in fact, under water. From the plane, the water was not at first easily discernible, for the ground could be seen beneath its surface. But the sun's reflection gave the game away, as it shone on the water covering the land, and the awful realisation came to me that an enormous area from Calcutta to Amritsar was waterlogged. It was not the dramatic flooding, which by its ravages and trail of death gets itself into the newspapers of the world, but a more sinister terror. Waterlogged land slowly disappears from cultivation and crops decline, while an increasing population demands an increased output. It is a grave menace to India's future and one that will demand much greater consideration.

Captain Singh Dugal and I had introduced ourselves, and after a preliminary 'bout', which included politics, it was easy to hear about the man himself. He told me that he was in the Artillery and pointed to his shoulder flash, indicating that all I had to do to identify an Indian soldier's corps was to prefix an 'R' to the initials. And so it was easy to deduce that an Indian bearing 'AMC' was in the equivalent of the Royal Army Medical Corps. A conversation such as that inevitably leads the Indian to deal with the links between Britain and India. The officers' mess is still the very traditional and stately affair it was in bygone days, with spirits flowing in the same profusion, for the forces are allocated special imports and at special prices. And the topic of drink led to a quaint story about the official daily ration of rum, to which Indian soldiers serving at stations above 7,000 feet are entitled. A delegation of MPs, who looked askance at this rule in an India that was endeavouring to become a prohibitionist country, was to visit one of these corps in the Himalayas. They arrived in the bitter cold of a 9,000 feet cantonment and undertook tours of inspection to keep them occupied for the days they were there before eventually returning to Delhi to make their report. As the report was taking a long time in preparation, enquiries were made about it. So the story goes, it was eventually discovered that the bitter cold and boredom of the cantonment had resulted in the delegation being added to the issue list for daily rum, and so the Indian army maintains this privilege.

Then there was the Bengali gentleman, who, as we picked our feet together, went into reminiscent mood, yearning for a stable society as exists in England – an England he had never seen. He turned out to be a haulage contractor. In other words, he had a fleet of lorries which went hither and thither all over the country. His problem, apparently, was the police. He complained about the very heavy 'levy' he had to pay in order to get his trucks passed at the regular 'roadworthiness' tests of commercial vehicles. As I was only too well aware of the lumbering wrecks that frequent Indian roads and serve as commercial transport, I understood his plight. But it was the recurrent expenditure that troubled him; he claimed that to avoid being hauled to court ad nauseam for trivial or non-existent offences, it was necessary to 'tip' the police in his home area. Whilst there was no regular scale laid down by law, Rs 2 per vehicle per month per constable was acceptable, and a somewhat heavier levy was acceptable by the inspector. This, as he pointed out, was an expense that had to be passed on to the customer and thereby increased costs generally.

I should say that many of the practices that are regarded by the West as 'corruption' are not seen in that light. It is so much a part of life that the young man, contemplating his career, sees his 'emoluments' in the police not as the Rs 60 or 90 (£7) per month, which he will be paid by the state. He will assess his income on the traditional 'perks', such as the scheme outlined by my Bengali friend, and indeed, the conception is closely akin to the young man in the West today who considers not only the salary offered, but the car provided, luncheon vouchers and expenses.

As we travel on through the day, parts of the country are revealed as being free of water and a more normal pattern of life is discernible in the fields we pass. India will never be deforested in any event, not completely, for there will always be one tree per holding. And the reason? Come the heat of midday, bullock and man must find shelter and the village is too far away. So it is siesta time under the neem tree, which fortunately never loses its leaves in the intense heat. And there he drinks from the earthenware bowl he brought along with him in the morning. It is amazing how cool the water has kept all day. He may have brought his hookah with him for a smoke, but in any event he will sleep the dead hours of heat away until the sun begins to sink in the west and the air loses its claustrophobic heat. As the evening grows closer, the peasants yoke up their oxen to the wooden plough. The word 'plough' is used despite the false impression the Western farmer may get, for it consists merely of a long stick dragged between the oxen, at the tip of which is another at right angles which does the 'ploughing'. That is the Indian plough, and were the noise of the train to cease for a moment we would hear the peasant shouting at his team to urge them on or just singing contentedly to himself.

Dinner that evening was very good: of curry and rice, a three-course meal for about two shillings. It is unwise to order a Western-type meal, for what one receives is considerably different from what one anticipated – or even ordered. I had ordered my dinner at one station and had it delivered at the next, and so on its arrival it was piping hot and just ready to be eaten. The bearer collected the dirty dishes at the next halt. And so to bed and time to lock up. Doors and windows are bolted against possible intruders at the night stops and the bedrolls shed their contents. These remarkable holdalls house a light mattress, pillow, sheets and, if necessary, a blanket. (You will remember that the pyjamas have already been in use all day.) There is also room for your clothes, but they will bear the scars of this form of travel until they can meet up with an iron.

Surprise, surprise. My first glimpse of Bengal reveals hills and undulating country, a feature seldom associated with Bengal's rice fields. There are many more trees, for we are closer to the sea and further now from the deserts of the northwest. But we are now entering the major industrial state of India. West Bengal (East Bengal is now Bangladesh) and its neighbour Bihar, through which we passed during the night, are the producers of coal and iron and boast the mighty steelworks of Jamshedpur, Durgapur and Rourkela. The latter two, with Bhilai in Madhya Pradesh, were constructed with assistance from Britain, West Germany and Russia respectively, and the race to complete the first project has been a source of great interest amongst Indians. And so the towns we pass through show signs of expanding industrialisation: Dhanbad, with its coalfields, provides an attraction to industry of the sort which brought prosperity to Lancashire in the 19th century. And with industry we see housing 'colonies' or estates for the workers. No flowers or trees, I am afraid, but nevertheless brick dwellings, each with their own courtyard and space separating them. But there are the exceptions – the main impression is one of slag heaps and industrial refuse, of abjectly poor people scavenging in the slag heaps and by the side of the railway line for anything passengers may have thrown out. The slight rise and fall of the land is further scarred by the hacking out of sand for building, which goes hand in hand with industry, and the brick kilns with their pathetic donkeys nearby. The squalor is disconcerting and disappointing to the traveller who holds belief in the values of industrialisation.

As we near Calcutta, the traditional Bengal scene reveals itself; the land of rice fields, a land of brilliant green – a well-worked green – and a people who are infinitely poorer than their brethren further west. And so into Howrah Station, Calcutta, and the terminus of the railway on the west side of the Hooghly River, hard by the great metal Howrah Bridge, which every Indian recognises as the symbol of Calcutta, as we associate the Tower Bridge and London.

Most people have a national sport – perhaps it is cricket or football or judo. India's is hockey (a good second place is held by cricket), but India is also a big country with federal states making up the whole. And while it may be inaccurate to define Bengal's national sport – or pastime – nevertheless, for Calcutta, tram burning must surely be named as a provincial hobby. The publicist uses it as his gauge of public opinion: the more trams that are burned, the greater is the degree of seriousness of the problem. These trams are owned by a British concern, but it is not because of that that they are used to draw off the steam of Calcutta's rioters. Today, with a long tradition of tram burning, it is said that Calcutta's Corporation dare not take the trams off the road – it may instead be the councillors' houses that receive the attentions of the rioters. And I should emphasise that the motive for the burnings need bear no connection with the innocent tram – perhaps it is the Chinese on the border, an invasion of Egypt or anything else you like to name.

For the Englishman, however, coming to Calcutta from Delhi, other reflections also assail him. Calcutta is very English. Yes – walk by the side of the Dakuria lakes, which is in a comparable position to Hyde Park in the heart of London, on a gusty, cloudy Sunday afternoon in September, and you will see the tall green trees blowing in the wind and the white-skinned rowing crews pulling over the rippled water. And in the distance the clubhouse, behind whose walls you will know are being practised the same drinking habits as are carried on in England. Or – you traveller from dusty Delhi – stand at the edge of the maidan (park) bordering Chowringhee, Calcutta's main shopping street, and one is reminded of Hyde Park and Park Lane. Add to this the Victoria memorial and the Anglican cathedral close by – all of these frequented by a fair proportion of Calcutta's British population in their white shirts and ties. But then the illusion is shattered; one's eyes focus on the beggars who have crept up on the wide Chowringhee, which serves as an impromptu race track for taxi drivers and bus drivers, and the decrepit traffic bears no resemblance to that of Park Lane – apart from the common element of an internal combustion engine, and frequently even that appears dubious.

The people who live in Calcutta are not only Bengalis. It is a cosmopolitan city which houses many Chinese and a large proportion of India's three million Anglo-Indians. It is the magnet which draws Orissans and Biharis to it with the great lure of Rs 30 or 40 per month. And a more subtle attraction is that the Harijans – or Untouchables – can lose the stigma of their lowly status in the anonymity of the big city. Thus thousands migrate to the slums of Calcutta, leaving their families behind in the village to till the land to secure a second source of income. These immigrants are popular with employers and householders, whose first question to the job and flat hunter will be, "Are you a Bengali?" If you can answer, "No. I am an Orissan," then you will be welcomed, for the Bengali is talkative and politically minded – to others this is translated as lazy and argumentative. Indeed, my host and his family enjoyed the discussion of my programme to the full and after an hour of its consideration I became embarrassed by such devoted attention to my welfare. On voicing this to my Bengali friend, he pointed out that as much joy was to be found in these preliminaries as in the activities themselves – I was fearful lest the latter should prove a terrible anti-climax!

Bengal is the land of the dhoti and Calcutta is its capital. No other garment can appear so repulsive as the dhoti, yet it is worn at virtually all social levels, and even those Bengalis conditioned to trousers for a spell of study in the West revert to the dhoti, almost without exception. Indeed, nobody can say that the Bengalis are slavish copiers of the West; their educated wives will still wait until their husbands have finished their meal before starting themselves. Yet from this land of the ghastly dhoti, most of India's film actresses come. The women of Bengal are among the finest and most beautiful of India and leave their menfolk far behind.

You can get anything in Calcutta, from a BA degree in the vernacular to a white woman for the night. But the item which most Bengalis struggle to acquire is the simple and straightforward bowl of rice, for we are no longer in the wheat-eating north but in the land of the rice field. Here in Bengal, rice grows abundantly in the green paddy fields, so well endowed with water. And the villagers emerge from their thatch-roofed, plaited bamboo-walled huts (mud huts would disintegrate in no time in this wet clime) to till their overcrowded lands. The poverty of these people is infinitely greater than that of the northerners – few are able to afford the odd bullock, which would provide them with a supply of milk for sale in nearby

Calcutta. Yet it is upon this Indian state that the additional burden of refugees from East Pakistan fell. Conversely, it is fortunate that West Bengal and its neighbour, Bihar, are receiving considerable assistance in the building up of heavy industry, and steel plants are going up in order to exploit the resources of coal to be found in the area. It will be a long struggle, however, before the lot of the Bengali can be raised to that of the Punjabi.

CHAPTER 6

KASHMIR

The great difficulty for the writer on Asia is to put things into a perspective recognisable to English or Western readers. And in doing so, one gives a false impression immediately, for Indian life is outside the range of experience of that reclusive gentleman – the average Englishman. And so it is with some trepidation that I stick my neck out and call Kashmir the Lake District of India. Having said that, let me say that nothing is further from the truth, apart from the fact that both Kashmir and the Lake District are in the north of their respective countries. Indeed, that statement is likely to cause trouble, for as you know, Pakistan claims Kashmir as hers and has held a sizeable portion of the area since the war of 1947–8. My journey was undertaken from Delhi, although the impact of the war between the two countries had a bearing on my travels, as will be seen. Now Kashmir can be reached by a daily air service, or by surface travel – I decline to use the term 'road', which conjures up a vision far removed from the reality. Moreover, surface travel can only be undertaken in summer – snow isolates the area in winter – and anyhow, who would want to leave the plains of north India in the beautiful weather of winter? So, you will immediately appreciate that I, the would-be traveller, wondered how to get out of the intense summer heat of the plains as quickly as possible. Should I travel by day the 400 miles to the point where the route enters the cool hills, thereby getting a 'normal' night's rest, or by night, thus avoiding the 100°F plus, which the temperature reaches shortly after dawn? A good old English compromise is reached, and the journey starts at about 5 p.m. And in order to make the best of one's holiday, it is Friday afternoon.

The car has been thoroughly serviced; new tyres are fitted, on the recommendation of the tourist people, to deal with the 'natural road surfaces' and spares of this, that and the other are loaded. An icebox –

in which the ice is already melting – holds liquid refreshment, which will be desperately needed within an hour. And so I enter my mobile hot house – or rather furnace – and hold the red-hot driving wheel gingerly as I start off. Not with the windows down, but slightly open, for otherwise I would find myself completely dehydrated by the dry air. An uneventful but tiring drive as the sun declines, the villagers returning to their homes as the light fades, slowing down my progress with their cumbersome bullock carts. And as night rapidly closes about the car, the headlights have the audacity to pick out the backsides of residents who come out from every village to answer their calls of nature by the roadside in the privacy afforded by the darkness. So now you will appreciate the additional use of the dipswitch in tropical climates... Only 120 miles that evening, and the reason for the low mileage is clear from the trucks which have come to grief – it is a straight road to Ambala - the sort of road on which the headlights of the truck approaching are in your eyes for about five miles. It is a tedious journey and sleep is liable to overcome even the most alert.

At Ambala a rest house awaits, and a meal, and a shower, and a servant to make up your bed. Breakfast in the morning will be thrown in and the whole lot comes to less than ten shillings. But the sun is up and as usual the good intentions of an early start have been to no avail. In any event, I swear not to stop before covering 100 miles. This portion of the Grand Trunk Road, which links Calcutta and Peshawar, is the best. It is, after all, the strategic road to the Pakistan frontier and to Kashmir. Thus the number of 'Irish bridges' one is required to deal with is down to a minimum. But, you ask, what are Irish bridges? Imagine a steep hill; the road is leading down into a river valley; a concrete strip stretches across the bottom and then up the other side. There are, apparently, ponds on either side of the road in the hollow and usually some water on the road itself. Bridges are expensive, and anyhow, it is only in the monsoon, and after, that the river is in spate. During part of the year it is dry, although the melting snows from the nearby Himalayas may give some extra water in the spring. And so the authorities have cemented a portion of the river's bed so that vehicles can get across without the luxury of a bridge. Of course, the hazards of such crossings demand a slow speed – it is no use thinking you can gather speed on the downhill stretch to get you up the opposite slope. That would be a pity, for you would probably acquire a broken axle as the car slithered into, and out of, the potholes made by the river in flood or a broken differential from the great stones that have been swept onto the 'bridge' by the stream. And as you would probably find the water was a damned sight deeper than you anticipated, you just won't force yourself through in top gear – and to change gear in mid-stream, just like changing horses there in olden days, is fatal. And your next question – why Irish bridges? Your guess will probably be better than mine.

But the 'regulation' Irish bridge is only to be found in textbooks – the hazards of nature have been described; there are the hazards that man, in his ingenuity, devoted to other ends, can and does add. Thus the enterprising villager in times of drought will consider how to make use of that nice pool of water dammed on the upstream side of our 'bridge'. It is needless to remark that this person's particular strip of land is downstream of the bridge. He thus finds it necessary to hack a channel into that beautiful concrete to enable the water to flow – he clearly regards the Irish bridge as part of an irrigation project rather than a roadway – and his indignation is considerable when the passing traveller finds it necessary to block his little channel with stones and rubble in order to get four wheels across. But such little snags irk us no more on this strategic part of the Grand Trunk Road, and we nip along at a glorious pace, pausing to let a spot of air out of the tyres every so often to prevent them blowing up in the scorching heat. It is an uneventful run until we turn off at Jullundur and make for the frontier post of Pathankot. This stretch of road is not really of military value, and aware of this I shudder at the thought of the road's condition. The military road to the north runs from Amritsar, which is further to the west. Indeed, before partition, travellers to Kashmir would never dream of using the route along which I will take you. They went via Lahore and Rawalpindi and along a gently sloping road into the vale of Kashmir, hugging the course of the river. Floods, even static water, play havoc with a road, and when the stretch has dried out it is unlikely that any tarmac will remain. And so one has to travel warily along the ridges of dirt thrown up by previous traffic – it is fatal for a private car's gearbox and sump to get caught in the tracks made by lorries and buses before you! But a few of these delays are less than an hour, and it is with great relief to find the nearest tea stall and, waving away the flies and maggoty dogs, to partake of that greatest of all drinks. At Pathankot it is wise to ask the state of the road. You will, no doubt, be informed that it is good, and in reply to your enquiry as to how many private cars are going through to Kashmir – still 200 miles away – you will be amazed by the knowledge that yesterday – or was it the day before? – one went through.

Why worry – there is every facility, rest houses erected and meals provided by a solicitous Kashmir Government to take care of the every need of travellers! And having written a fortnight before to book in at one of these establishments, I hadn't a care in the world. At least until the official told me that the road out of Jammu – still 60 miles away – closed for traffic at 6 p.m., and it was then 3.30 p.m. As luck would have it, my rest house was 20 miles the other side of Jammu. So let's go, but with little hope. To my amazement, the road was excellent in parts – a double track road, but jammed with military convoys, for the road further along had given way. All traffic had been halted and had been piling up for several days. This I did not know until later – all I was aware of was that every vehicle in India must be in my way. By confining myself to the right-hand side of the road – fortunately the trucks were all going, not coming – I managed to get to Jammu just in time. I was the last to clear the checkpoint, where they take name and number, so that if you don't arrive at the rest house, they know you've tumbled off the precipitous mountain road...

Now the journey had really entered its worst. Leaving Delhi and arriving in the Valley of Kashmir, you have to cross five rivers. All of you will clearly remember from schooldays the great rivers that irrigate the north-western plains of the subcontinent; as you travel north, first the Sutlej then the Beas, the Ravi, the Chenab, and at Srinagar itself, the Jhelum. Only the mighty Indus is not crossed. Thus if you cannot see the implications, let me tell you that it means crossing mountain ridge after mountain ridge. Only between Sutlej and Beas do you traverse level ground. But it is dark and I feel surprise at the relative ease of the journey, and only later do I realise the nature of my fool's paradise. My headlights could not pick out the floors of the enormous chasms which edged the road all the way. At one corner it was necessary to back almost over the edge in order to circumnavigate its sharpness. And so I reached Kud, 7,000 feet above sea level, where the former prime minister of Kashmir was imprisoned – surely the most beautiful surroundings to bless any political prisoner. And then to my rest house at Batote to find that they had not received my booking – it was being 'processed' by 'head office', which explained the delay of many bookings. However, a room was available; a fire was not. The temperature was now about 60°F lower than earlier in the day, and at 55°F I was shivering. In the stillness of the evening I ate my curry and rice and gazed in awe at the myriad of lights from the fires of the military in their tiny camps dotted all over the mountains, guarding the road to Kashmir. I determined to be up at dawn to get my first glimpse of this beautiful land and to make an early start.

I was awake at dawn – I was awake long before with the roar of military traffic on the road below my window. Surely this was it – I was caught up in some new invasion. I and my Indian-built Hindustan Landmaster car would never get out. It was pointless to get up at dawn other than to admire the scenery – the tourist office had omitted to tell me of the convoy system that was in operation over the vast stretch of road; the next 50 miles to the great Banipal Tunnel. And the 'up' traffic was not scheduled to start until midday. In any event, the problem remained of getting ahead of 150 army lorries – a privilege accorded to the one or two tourist cars which dare the journey. This, incidentally, is a blessing, for inevitably the road gives way under the terrific pounding of this mass of military traffic and if you are in the rear you will be stranded. At twelve o'clock the army major in charge of the convoy advised us that the road was 'down' again and there would be further delay. I was thankful, for the effort to get in front of the convoy had left me nearly exhausted: on a road unfit for two vehicles to pass, I had to edge past 150 or more lorries on the right-hand side of the road. However, as traffic was coming out from Kashmir, I had frequently to back up along the edge of a precipice to find a space into which I could squeeze the car and let the oncoming traffic pass. On occasion I had to persuade a couple of army drivers to move their lorries a yard or two forward or backward to let me squeeze in out of the way.

The convoy comprised first an army jeep with hundreds of vehicles strung out behind us, including two tourist cars and, believe it or not, a couple of buses, and our speed was limited to ten miles per hour. Orders from the major were not to stop and to stay in the order dictated by him (as if you could do anything else), and he tactfully indicated that there were no public lavatories en route. To be in a convoy is nerve-racking, for you may wish to stop and let the engine cool, or you may wish to hold a certain speed so that you don't have to drop down to bottom gear. But of the need for the convoy system there was no doubt. Above us towered five to ten thousand feet of mountain; below us was a further 3,000 feet of fresh air. There we were, perched on this minute ledge, sometimes struggling upward, sometimes travelling precipitously downwards, and all the time turning corners of nerve-racking sharpness – the term 'hairpin' I do not use, for it is an understatement – all the while on a surface a goat would think twice about using. But it was clear what the major's term 'road down' meant. It meant precisely that: that the tiny ledge, which is Kashmir's link with the outside world, had given way under the terrific pounding and disintegrated into the gorge beneath.

On occasion, a few tons of boulders and clay would tumble down from above and block the route. However, at the spots where this was likely to occur, a little nook was available, and out of it would emerge a bulldozer pushing the debris off the edge to tumble into the chasm far below. You will understand from this that boundary walls to this road are regarded as an irrelevant luxury. The bridges we crossed were all armed; only one vehicle at a time was allowed on, and the leading jeep, once across, would wait patiently to ensure that the tourists got across without plunging to their deaths – the army men following were left to their fate. Some of the bridges were of wood, and the tree trunks used as uprights would groan fearfully under the weight. I needed no second bidding to delay my crossing until the vehicle in front got across!

Inevitably, the worry, and the earlier cups of tea, did their work and I had to stop my car. And the whole convoy stopped behind me as I dashed behind a projecting boulder – modesty was utterly impossible – and the major dashed back to see what was holding up the convoy. But after that I felt better, and the tortuous ups and downs – two or three thousand feet a time – gave way to a steady downhill drive, into the town of Banihal. It had taken five hours to cover 50 miles. I learned that the road had collapsed twice behind us and the end portion of the convoy would be stuck there for 12 hours at least. But do not think that this was an end to the journey – we had still to navigate the highest of all – the 8,000-feet high Banihal pass and tunnel. At the checkpoint, free of the convoy, your details are once again taken and phoned up to the tunnel. I was reluctant to carry more weight than necessary, so I decided not to fill up at the next petrol station – a very dangerous proceeding in India, and very much more so in Kashmir, where the next petrol available may be a very long way off. It was a good road and a serviceable tunnel, one mile long with water pouring from the unlined roof and, of course, pitch dark. At the other end was the Vale of Kashmir – 150 miles inside the colossal mountain barrier of the Himalayas, with one of the finest climates on earth. It is indeed isolated, and linked by this all too valuable lifeline with the outside world. The valley is 50 miles long and 20 wide and supports nearly three million people, representing three-quarters of Kashmir's population. All its produce goes out by our dirt-track route – the wood, for which it is famous, no longer travels down the River Jhelum to Rawalpindi's sawmills, for that way lies Pakistan. Instead it is taken in groaning trucks to Amritsar and the plains of India. Likewise, all supplies coming in, military and civilian petrol, food, cement, munitions and clothing, must use the route. All come through the 200 miles of mountain passes, ridges and ledges to emerge in what might be described as a freak of nature concealed in the depths of the mighty Himalayas.

It is an easy trip into Srinagar from the tunnel, with the road lined by tall and slender poplars reminiscent of parts of France. The slopes of the valley itself are densely forested and it is curious to observe the absence of wooden dwellings in such a land. But the trees are a state monopoly, as they were of the Maharajah in earlier days, and thus the villagers must construct their homes with mud and bricks.

And so to Srinagar, Kashmir's beautiful capital on the shores of the Jhelum River and Dal and Nagin lakes. And just look at it – the incredible floating gardens, the wonderful houseboats, and the romantic shikaras. Do not bother to go further than the lakes. To go into the city is to experience a degree of disillusionment. There are too many soldiers about, and the Sikh police belie the fact that you are in a country very different from the one you left in the plains. They are Muslims, these Kashmiris, and are proud of their Kashmir. They provide for the tourist a degree of comfort and gracious living in the houseboats on the lakes that is unknown elsewhere in India. The carpets are thick, the ornaments profuse, the boats spotless, the food magnificent and the service excellent. "If there be a heaven here on earth, it is here. It is here." The words were those of a Moghul emperor, but they are echoed by virtually every foreigner who stays isolated on a houseboat, with the graceful shikaras – a gondola which puts those of Venice in the third-rate category – as his link with the outside world and in which to explore the floating gardens. But inevitably, in order to provide this venue of wonder for the tourist there is a way of life which contrasts terribly with that of the tourist. You will see the women in their tiny kayak-like canoes, searching for weed growing from the bottom of the lakes, and she who finds a piece of floating garden – even six inches square – is overjoyed. They take their proceeds back and extend their own floating garden with them. I am told that more than 100,000 people live on the tiny solid islands in the lakes and that there is no land for them apart from the spaces their homes occupy. But the lakes do provide an alternative in the form of a weed that grows from the lake's shallow bottom, which will support a flourishing market garden industry. On these floating gardens, peas, tomatoes and the like are grown for sale in Srinagar. Of course, root crops cannot be grown, nor maize or rice, and it is a bone of contention with the 'islanders', who claim that they should be given land on which to grow the food which makes up their own diet. To stand on the floating gardens is possible but precarious, for they sink almost a foot beneath the surface – rather like trying to stand on an air-bed floating on the water. The floating gardens are tended by the women-folk in their tiny craft while the men work in Srinagar for the tourist, primarily plying shikaras or taxi scooters.

Do not go to Gulmarg – it just is not worth it to see what most resembles a derelict American gold-rush town, with its wooden bungalows rapidly falling to bits. It is from this elevated position, only 20 miles from Srinagar, that Pakistan guns controlled a large section of the valley in the war of 1947–8. It is no use talking about 'The War' in Kashmir if you are thinking of the activities of 1939–45, for here in this lovely valley that escapade did not touch them. But in 1947 they learnt what war was, for the guns were firing on Srinagar itself as the Maharajah made a hectic dash for safety to Indian territory, where he has remained in exile ever since. Indeed, five miles outside Srinagar the stately poplars are not so tall – they are newly planted to replace those destroyed during the war and are only now achieving a modest stature.

And so the days pass in luxurious idleness – if you want a drink or if you want to join the American tourists, you can visit the Palace Hotel overlooking the Dal Lake. But why bother, for on the placid waters your houseboat rocks almost imperceptibly, and the stillness of the evening is disturbed only by the swish of a passing shikara or by the cracking of the fire which is being prepared to cook your evening meal. Even this will not disturb the exquisite tranquillity of a Kashmir evening, for the cooking is done on an adjacent, smaller houseboat on which the owner and his family live. Yes, they know the English – before 1947, Srinagar and its houseboats were packed, but now there are fewer visitors, and so you can have an eight-roomed (or is it cabined?) houseboat to yourself, and all for £2 per day.

Perhaps you are not satisfied with the site. No? Well then we will have the houseboat moved, and father and son will punt this huge 50-year-old craft to wherever you wish – limited only by the local bye-laws and the availability of an electricity connection with the shore. Needless to say, your arrival has not been unobserved. Apart from the tourist office, which wants your opinion of the place, and the police who want your passport number, the many merchants of Srinagar will have acted upon the assumption that you want at least 50 per cent of their stock. Thus you will find that instead of being alone the following morning, breakfast is served by a harassed bearer who is under specific instructions not to let anyone aboard. The water is dotted with a multitude of boats, whose owners will sell you postcards, paintings, cutlery, blankets, carpets, cigarettes, table lamps, groceries and tinned goods, shirts and suits. Members of the group will be prepared to make you a suit in two days, take your photograph, hire you a speedboat for water-skiing, shave you, take you on a tour of the town, provide you with feminine companionship, and try to persuade you that their houseboat is much better and much cheaper. The chances are you'll buy a box of matches and suggest they return in a few days' time – the calculation based on your number of days' sojourn in Kashmir plus one. In actual fact, your bearer will be getting a backhander from those traders he recommends, but nonetheless, it is worthwhile to accept his advice. Why not order a carpet to be made for you to your own pattern, as if you were a woman choosing a pattern for a dress you wanted made up? And in the process you will be offered tea and sweetmeats, which you will accept or refuse, depending upon your fear of dysentery.

The days pass – brilliant sunshine every day, but not too hot, and cool evenings and crisp nights – until the time comes to leave the valley. You have got used to awakening to see the snow-capped ridges of the Himalayas high up in the sky, yet not so far away. You have almost forgotten the smells of the dirty road and of the car's engine and upholstery. But it must end and you ascertain the times of the convoys, only to be told that the convoy system hasn't been used for years! The gentleman concerned was not so much interested in my welfare as a tourist but in the welfare of his son, and he saw a remote opportunity of getting him into an English university – fees, travel and maintenance paid, of course. Having been obliged to disillusion the said gentleman to the fact that I myself was not the United Nations Technical Assistance Bureau, I left the office none the wiser about the times of the convoys. The military were again courteous on the road back and the journey presented fewer of the problems of the outward journey, apart from the one ghastly rest house. I was deluded by its situation beside a fast-flowing stream of perfectly clear mountain water set in a valley crowded with rhododendrons in flower, which are, incidentally, natives of the Himalayas. The chowkidar (watchman) let me in but indicated the presence of scorpions and snakes on the premises. He furthermore provided me with a stick to beat the latter to death. I am still not certain whether he intended this warning as a deterrent to giving him any trouble by my stopping there, but it threatened a sleepless night, for there were many strange noises which demanded investigation at frequent intervals before I could even think it fit to lie down. Finally, I blocked all possible snake entrances and in blissful forgetfulness of the huge chimney by my head, fell asleep exhausted.

It was not many miles further on that the hot plains of India hit car and driver. And 'hit' is the right word to describe the furnace heat that greets the Kashmir-fresh tourist, and by the time Delhi, 200 miles further on, was reached, the beneficial effects of the Kashmir holiday were reduced to nil.

CHAPTER 7

HILL STATIONS

During the English winter, the wealthy retreat to the south of France to find a spot where the temperature is somewhat higher and to where there is extra sunshine. The foreigner in India – as well as the Indian himself – occasionally feels he wants a little less sunshine and a few degrees Fahrenheit or Centigrade less. This period is apt to be about April when the great land-mass of the subcontinent begins to warm up and continues warming up until the monsoon brings welcome relief with heavy rains. But from April to the end of June, Delhi, like the rest of north India, can experience temperatures well over the 100°F mark, and in June the night temperature is almost the same. Indeed, late at night, any metal surface is still fiercely hot and even to lie back in the bath sends no shudder through you, for the bath itself, despite the 'cold' water, is warm. Tempers fray with the increasing temperature and life becomes very trying. This is the time when most people endeavour to get away into the hills. The 'hills' are the ridge of the Outer Himalayas, which stretch the whole length of north India and rise to a height of about eight to nine thousand feet.

They say that Darjeeling is the best hill station, which people from Calcutta visit, but I will have to take their word for it, as I have never been there. The tourist office incautiously boasts its merits by suggesting rising at sunrise to see the sun appear over Everest – or is it Kanchenjunga? At the other end of Nepal lie the hill stations serving the northern plains (few of these 'stations' boast platforms, never mind trains). From Delhi you have a choice of Naini Tal, Mussoorie or Simla. These are the main centres, although there are others, smaller or further away. Why would you choose one and not the others? Let us tentatively propose Naini Tal, and having done so we find that it is 220 miles away, but the snag is the River Ganges. You can get across the Jumna all right, and one or two other rivers –

nipping over the combined road and rail bridges while the rail signals are at danger, for the trains that is – but the Ganges has not yet been bridged for road traffic. That is not to say that the traveller by road has been ignored. As it is the dry season, the river is but a trickle instead of its normal four miles width at Garmukhteshar and only about 200 yards wide. Wonderful, you say. Well, not quite, for the watery stretch is the easiest part, as pontoons have been flung across in true military style and you waddle from boat to boat over the improvised roadway. It is on either side of this facility that there are difficulties and you must come prepared to devote an hour or two to the operation. First, of course, you find it is dead easy – it is just like any other unmade road, finding potholes with every revolution of the wheels. But then comes the sand and once again you have been taken care of, for on the sand have been laid steel plates for the wheels to ride over. Fine; get on them and you find that with the weight of the car, the other end of the plate pops up a mere six feet away, which in turn lifts the blunt end of the next plate, menacing your headlights or your tyres. The secret is to go slowly – yes, very slowly – for any attempt at speed will have you minus your engine sump or plus a couple of ripped tyres. You dare not leave the plates or you will never get out of the sand without the help of a couple of bullock carts. Add to all this your boiling engine in bottom gear and the temperature of about 115°F.

So without more ado we decide to avoid Naini Tal. But first of all, let us take a look at what we have missed. A beautiful climb of 20 miles up to 6,000 feet above sea level to the lake of Naini, where you can sail to your heart's content, where you can play golf on the very English 18-hole course, where you can send your children to the finest schools in India or elsewhere. If you wish, you can move on to Ranikhet 50 miles away, another hill resort with a constant view of the mighty snow-bedecked Himalayas, stretching as far as the eye can see. And there are other spots, such as Bim Tal and Nakutchiatal, with its magnificently transparent lake, barely accessible by car, where you can enjoy the most stimulating bathing in the sub-continent.

And there is not a soul to disturb you except perhaps the ghost of Jim Corbett, the great tiger hunter who lived nearby. Where to stay? Do not stay at the hotels – please! You will be disappointed unless you are yearning for a typical English seaside hotel of the 1890s. If that is your wish, you will have found your dream, for in your hotel you will find metal-ended beds raised about four feet from the ground – ground rather than floor because the cement is clearly visible through the threadbare carpets. Undoubtedly, the furniture has endured – thanks to the excellence of Victorian craftsmen – from the 1890s or thereabouts. If I were taking bets, I should say that the decorations were last done in celebration of the Golden Jubilee of Queen Victoria, although one or two patching jobs were undertaken in the reign of King Edward VII. There are photographs of those distinguished monarchs all over the place. I am not sure if the proprietors are aware of the accession to the throne, never mind the death of King George VI. It is not necessary to add that Indian independence has passed them by. They will be anxious to do all they can for you, and the Anglo-Indian proprietor will show you the remainder of the establishment's somewhat inadequate facilities and a servant will start wiping the dust from the washbowl on the dresser in your room. But they can do nothing about the springs in the sofa – they were put there by the makers and extracting them would leave you sitting on the floor. Nevertheless, you remain uncomfortably aware of their presence. Don't bring your electric razor, for you will find a technical difficulty – no electricity, so please do not embarrass the management with enquiries about voltage.

At dinner you will be reminded that you are in India – the bearer is bare-footed and carefully serves wishy-washy Western food in his scruffy white coat. In any event, you will not be alone, for joining you from time to time are the jolly little mice who belt across the room, presumably visiting their mates in one of the many access holes designed for this purpose. A gloomy picture? Perhaps, but remember that we have decided not to visit Naini Tal anyway. What about Simla – the spot that ranks with Poona in the minds of Kipling fans and music hall jokers and which, incidentally, is the present day capital of the centrally administered state of Himachel Pradesh?

The Government is worried about these hill stations. Since the British left, their purpose in life has declined and the Indians have devised an ingenious method of keeping then alive. They set up military staff centres, administration, research and training establishments in what they might term 'depressed areas'. In these towns "fings ain't what they used to be", but Simla still is a gem. It is 60 miles by road from the plains and the railway line boasts the defeat of the stiff gradients in 120 miles. You can choose to go by bus, leaving your car at the bottom, and the excitement is intense. The buses, of course, have no windows, this being a dual-purpose idea – to let the breeze in and to let sick people lean out. Get a window seat whatever you do and then enjoy the view, which normally starts six inches away from the wheels of the bus and drops away – hundreds of feet to begin with and thousands of feet the nearer you get to Simla. Actually, you can see Simla soon after leaving the plains, but the bus is no helicopter and must stick to the tortuous road, which puts many a roller coaster to shame.

Once in Simla, head for the rest house, where no doubt you have already arranged accommodation. Having unpacked, walk along the Mall – where once upon a time Indians were not allowed – to the English church at the end. Services are still held for the Anglo-Indian community and the visitors. The tourist trade is catching hold of the idea of inducing people to come to Simla in the winter. A difficult job, but they are aided and abetted by the heavy snows which cover these mountains in winter. And so you can have your white Christmas right there in India, with genuine Christmas trees, tobogganing and skiing, plus church service on Christmas morning. Incredible? Yes, it is, particularly the charges for skiing. Grab an instructor – graciously provided from one of India's crack mountain brigades – skis and all the equipment you need, spend the morning on the ski slopes under the soldier's expert guidance and you will be out of pocket to the tune of about seven shillings. If this 'plug' does not send you flocking to the Indian slopes instead of Switzerland, I can at least inform you that it does bring good souls from as far away as the Persian Gulf and Malaya.

The facilities of this summer resort include golf, tennis and horse riding for all, which is a good idea considering that everything is either up or down, but never along the horizontal. Moreover, you have to leave your car outside the town. You can also enjoy the occasional dance band that takes the opportunity of emerging from Delhi's heat. Or the cinema – I should mention that you have a choice between English and American films (those made in the late 30s and early 40s now being shown) and Indian films. If you go to the latter, prepare to spend a couple of hours, but do not imagine that all the dialogue will be incomprehensible, for the heritage of the English language is such that you will understand certain snippets – 'blast', 'damn', 'my God', 'shut up' and many others will have a familiar ring throughout the performance...

It is near Simla that you take the picture of the year. A few miles outside the town you join the road to Tibet. Once again, the term 'road' is a misnomer, but it is a track used by buses, brigands and coolies and on it you find the milestone 'Tibet 190 miles'. Near this point you come across a curious reminder of the war. It is a rest house which has an excellent library of thrillers, a legacy of the time it was a rest centre for troops coming out of Burma. Situated atop an 8,000-foot peak, it commands stupendous views of the Himalayas and of the mighty Sutlej River gorge. Yet surrounding it are peaceful gardens and pine trees. It even boasts its own water supply, pumped thousands of feet up from the river below, purified and then served in buckets! To such places come few foreigners nowadays and many Indians. This rest house, Carignanon, is visited by the President of India and his family.

Another spot that many Delhi-wallas favour is Mussoorie. At a distance of 180 miles, it is Delhi's closest hill station and the easiest drive. The road is quite good, all single track of it, and not particularly liable to flooding. If you must, you can reach Mussoorie 'direct' from Simla. The distance is a mere 150 miles, but I assure you it is worth the detour, almost back to Delhi – 300 miles – to get there. Assuming you wish to go direct, you will travel surely the most dangerous stretch of road in India, with hairpin bends on one in four gradients, cleverly combined with 3,000-foot drops if you move an inch in the wrong direction on the mass of slate and stones digni-fied by the term 'road'. It is in recognition of one or two of these shortcom-ings that a 50-mile stretch is limited to westbound traffic until 3 p.m., east-bound until dusk. There is not a drop of petrol to be had for 100 miles, and when you are fairly safely down the hills, you have to be ferried across the turbulent Jumna on a very rickety boat, which rolls perilously under the weight of the car.

Forget this trip. We will sensibly leave from Delhi. You can combine a most interesting visit to the Holy Ganges en route, through the lovely forest area of the Shiwalik Hills to Hardwar and Rishikesh, where the lifeblood of India – spiritually and agriculturally – emerges from the Himalayas. This is the Canterbury of India, apart from Benares, where the devout Hindu comes to worship and to meditate. The busy clerk from the government office in Delhi will come for a week's holiday with his wife simply to relax and, as they do at Blackpool, to bathe. It is true that the degree of worship to the sun goddess may be different, for the Indian has no need to acquire a tan as has his Blackpool counterpart. At night, the bereaved light tiny candles, float them on leaves and set them to drift down the river. It makes a serene and beautiful sight to see the myriad of lights moving slowly away, taking with them the reverence of relatives for the departed. But like most places, an attraction is commercially exploited. The minimum services command a large fee; the so-called holy men flock to squeeze the pilgrims. As one Indian told me, "We know that 90% are frauds, but how are we to determine which are genuine and which are not? So we must give to all, hoping that we are giving to the genuine." The town of Hardwar can boast one of the most squalid town centres on earth, and the prostitution trade flourishes for those who do not take their religious vacation too seriously.

And so to Dehra Dun, India's Sandhurst, where virtually all the offic-ers in the army have been trained. The Military Academy is run on British lines; indeed, the very buildings are reminiscent of an English 'institution' – of military training, of course. The Academy and the enormous num-bers of retired people who migrate to Dehra Dun after a life in government service or on the railways (may I call it also India's Bournemouth?) make it a prosperous town. Being just to the north of a range of hills it is saved from the torrid heat of the plains and enjoys a most equable climate, and is cheaper to live in than the hill stations above it. Some of the homes in the town are very fine indeed. They are bungalows situated in their own grounds, almost immersed in trees, rhododendrons, bougainvillea and a riot of greenery and bright flowers. A garden in this area can be a gardener's paradise. In the evenings you can sit out on the verandah and enjoy the nip of the evening air, as well as the nip of whisky – even if you cannot get real Scotch, try the Indian equivalent, which is similar to an Irish whiskey. Alternatively, try Indian beer, described as a lager, which has a kick twice as strong as the refreshment we understand to be lager!

While in Dehra Dun, visit the Forest Research Centre. Having visited it you will undoubtedly be inspired to acquire your qualifications in the art of forestry, whatever they might be, and immediately apply to the Indian Civil Service Commission. For the bungalows, which even relatively junior officers are allocated, are reminiscent of some of the elite homes in Windsor Great Park and the surroundings are of the same calibre. Let us leave Dehra Dun, past its sawmills and through the land apportioned to retired Gurkhas of the Indian army – whereas we have trouble getting people into the army, the Indians have trouble getting them out. They are allowed to serve for a limited period only and whilst they are in the army they get the best of attention and facilities. Their pay – the NCOs and privates – is rated in shillings per month, but the accommodation and food for themselves and their families are good. The facilities include everything from sport and films to education and voluntary sterilisation after a certain number of children. Who could want for more? It is not surprising that they are a little concerned about facing the hard facts of the Indian labour market. With the Gurkhas, who frequently have no home and piece of land to go back to, the problem is still more difficult. Here at Dehra Dun there is a colony of them, each with their little huts and piece of land and pretty slit-eyed children playing around, while their fathers cultivate some of the best rice grown in India. Tea is also grown in the Doon valley and provides a cash crop for many farmers.

A mile of two outside Dehra Dun the road begins sloping upwards, and before you realise it the arduous 15-mile hill stretch begins, involving driving up 5,000 feet to Mussoorie. As we leave the plains we leave the 100°F plus temperatures. Dusk is falling and as we climb the degrees are rapidly deducted. The road to Mussoorie is magnificent; it is a tarmac road capable of taking two streams of traffic. The 'cats'-eyes' on the road consist of ordinary builder's bricks sunk in the road surface at an angle of 45° and painted white – woe betide the tyres of those who ignore the doctrine 'keep to the left'. The rule of the road gives right of way to up-going traffic, which is sound sense. A toll is charged, for the cost of maintenance is enormous. Men are constantly on duty to report landslides, and when they occur the road is rapidly cleared for at least one-way traffic.

It is in the monsoon period that most landslides occur, when the water seeps into the ground, undermining unsound areas. At intervals, troughs are placed by the roadside, not so much for horses as for over-heated radiators. The pony traffic takes a different route – the old road, which was the only way up until 1926. Before that you hired a two-wheeled rickshaw and were pushed up the 5,000 feet and six miles into Mussoorie over an unmade road. Today, produce is still expensive in Mussoorie, for everything must come from the plains below; little cultivation can take place on the steep hillsides and only goats and some cattle are kept by the hill farmers for their milk. The cabbage you eat, the potatoes, the flour for your bread, and fruit all come from the plains in panniers strapped to the sides of ponies. Ten ponies will come up, herded by their owner, and the day's vegetables are distributed in the bazaar.

Communications in a hill station are of interest – normally the wheel is superfluous, whether it is for a pram or a bus. It just is not a practical proposition. For merchandise, the coolies from the mountains with their Mongoloid features will carry incredible loads for next to nothing. If you are in the Public Works Department and want great lengths of piping to be transported, the coolie will do it; if you are a school manager wanting the boys' luggage taken to the bus station, the coolie will carry it. He straps the load up – two or three trunks will do – sits down on the ground and gets the straps over his forehead; and his mate takes the weight of the load so that he can get to his feet. Thus, bent forward at 45°, he plods off in a foot covering of rags. The necks of many of these men are severely swollen from the fantastic strain imposed on their heads and they die early deaths from this, one of the worst ways in the world of making what is laughingly called a 'living'. The elite in the coolie world operate from the bazaars and the bus stops, carrying your odd half a dozen suitcases half a mile for about one shilling.

There are other items to be carried – yourself or your child for example. You will require four gents for your personal taxi service. Having decided on the outing, your bearer will call the chowkidar (watchman), who will start yodelling over the hillsides for his mates. They may be doing a spot of work on the pathways, perhaps repairing a part of the track which has slipped down the hillside and which in all probability they pushed in order to get the work repairing it! This procedure, incidentally, is sound economics for the employee, but the municipality and the ratepayer take a poor view of such imaginative enterprise. However, your gentlemen have arrived and you get into the dandy, which is a seat surrounded by canvas and suspended from two poles which are carried on the shoulders of the four men. For the baby, however, only one porter is needed and he carries a basket affair on his back, in which the child sits safely strapped in (we hope) with room for parcels underneath. The entourage departs for the town's shopping centre – the bazaar. It is a pleasant ride in the warm sunshine and you can rest assured that the youngster will be asleep very soon with the persistent jogging and the warmth.

Another interesting exercise for the intrepid communications expert is to drive a car up the steep slope in Landour bazaar. Engage bottom gear and don't stop. Regardless of whom or what is in the way, for it is so steep you will never start the car again. Unfortunately, it involves large numbers of shoppers having to step right through what would be the windows of the bazaar's shops and much confusion results. On occasion, however, it is necessary, for the hospital has been cleverly sited at the top of all this, presumably as a discouragement to hypochondriacs. The final lap of this marathon climb requires coaxing the car up and over a step built into the road for drainage purposes. It is one-way traffic without traffic lights, so I cannot give advice as to the action to be taken in the event of your coinciding your trip up with the other chap's descent.

I do not know the vital statistics of Mussoorie, but I can tell you it is 6,000 feet above sea level and that most of this is sheer drop, giving magnificent views of the plains to the south (on a clear day you can see points 80 miles away). To the other side of the ridge – 'saddle' is the correct term – on which the town is built, there are contrasting and even more inspiring views of the everlasting snows of the Inner Himalayas. I can tell you that Mussoorie's population is about ten times greater in summer than in winter, for not only do visitors depart but also the coolies, rickshaw men and traders, plus the semi-permanent residents of the town, who find their hill-top houses too cold during the winter. Despite all this, the town and its environs collect other nomads – hill panthers encroach upon the deserted gardens and somewhat reduce the dog population, which frequently is not a bad thing. However, the tourist handouts will explain that the best months to visit Mussoorie are April to June and September to October. This period curiously coincides with the worst pre- and post-monsoon weather in the plains. Your free leaflet will tell you that the maximum temperature in these months is 90°F and the minimum about 60°F. You will be enamoured by the magic of Mussoorie, the queen of the hill stations, and reminded of the patrons of old – Mussoorie was, and is, the hill station of the princes, as Simla was the hill station of the Government. This was intentional, for they did not want the intrigue of Delhi to continue in close proximity to Simla. Today, the summerhouses of the Maharajahs dot the hillsides and it is still a major expedition when one of these gentry decides to go on holiday. There is one gentleman who brings his 80 thoroughbred dogs, his armed guards and a couple of lorries and a jeep for his personal use, which he drives, in kid gloves, flying his 'national' flag.

The guidebook will not mention some of the tragic recent history of the place, the times of 1947, when some of the worst of the communal riots occurred in these hill stations; that in Mussoorie no Muslim was safe and the Government had to evacuate each and every one. Today, you may be shown the spot where a busload of Muslims being evacuated were deliberately driven over the precipice to their deaths by their non-Muslim driver, who jumped out just in time to save himself. Today, however, Muslims have returned and those with property have got it into shipshape order once again.

Instead of going to an hotel, hire a bungalow, which with four or five bedrooms and the other chambers associated with domestic architecture you will rent for about £2 a week. Hill servants, much dirtier, will cost you a mere £4 a month and the view will cost you nothing, although occasionally it disappears when a dust storm moves over the plains and the view is blotted out. Another curious feature of this existence is the impression one gets of being in an aeroplane. This is particularly so during the monsoon, when the masses of cloud press in on the plains some thousands of feet below your vantage point. And you can see the approach of the rain belt in time to get home – or to be warned to take your umbrella. Speaking of umbrellas, this is as necessary an implement of a hill servant's profession as the saw is to the carpenter. Indeed, the first question during the interview is not whether he can cook, but whether he has an umbrella. If he has not, he is either mad or a liar and will involve you in the immediate purchase of one for him. Even the milkman carries an umbrella – whose other attire consists of an old shirt, shorts (formerly longs but cut down) and the milk strapped in small churns onto his back. I feel that if the bowler-hatted, brolly-carrying gentry of London's fair city were to see their counterparts (umbrella carriers that is) in India's hills they would revert to pacamacs immediately. Of course, the umbrella is not carried immaculately rolled up when not in action, but in the fashion of a soldier shouldering arms. The ingenious alternative method is to hook the handle into the back of the shirt collar with a devil-may-care 'look, no hands' attitude, and from the front it also appears as 'look, no umbrella'.

The population of Mussoorie is mixed; there are not only Indians and visitors but also a big Anglo-Indian community. There are the occasional widows of British officials who have little to take them back to England and not a sufficiently large pension to enable them to live in comfort there. But in Mussoorie they have pretty little cottages surrounded by flowers and they keep a couple of cats or birds. Some of these gardens are a riot of colour and beauty and strike the new arrival fresh from England as 'more English than the English themselves'. The Anglo-Indian community is large; they work in the schools or are retired and live out their lives far from the rigours of the plains below, which some of them have not visited since independence. The schools in the hills are of some calibre. They were originally sited in the hills for health reasons and their clientele consisted of the children of expatriate officials and of the wealthier Anglo-Indians. The schools continue to maintain high standards combined with quite modest fees. They are supported financially by State Governments, but naturally most of their pupils now are Indians and there are certain requirements regarding the use of Hindi as the medium of instruction in addition to English.

Many Anglo-Indians cannot speak Hindi, or any Indian language. They are all Christians – indeed, all Indians professing Christianity are regarded as Anglo-Indians by their fellow countrymen. Nevertheless, there are over three million persons of mixed race, most of whom look upon England as 'home' and many have little tolerance of Indians. It is only recently that the girls began wearing the sari occasionally, in which most of them look infinitely finer than in Western dress. So often one hears, "I have to change at my friend's house, as Mummy would throw me out if she saw me in a sari." But this attitude is changing and the community – a protected one under India's constitution – is sensibly accepting and finding pride in Indian citizenship. Many of them go into the senior branch of the Civil Service, the army and navy and fly jets in India's air force. Their girls may be teachers, secretaries and air hostesses of Air India International.

But in Mussoorie we meet the older kind, rather resentful of any 'intrusion' when an Indian buys a house in their area, and like people in Britain, seldom speak to these neighbours of theirs. It is difficult not to feel sorry for some of these people, misfits in their own country and unable to live in England, which holds their loyalty and sentiment. They are staunchly British in outlook and many will go to great lengths to trace their ancestry in order to qualify for a United Kingdom passport and citizenship. For the younger ones, many are determined to get to England, where they feel they will be amongst their own kind. Some fit in well, but others are taken aback by Britons who inevitably regard them as coloured and unwittingly remark on how well they speak English!

And so life in Mussoorie progresses; the sunshine of June gives way to the torrential rain of the monsoon, when snakes are driven from their holes – but seldom enter the house – and when scorpions like to get cosily ensconced in the bedclothes. Long grass abounds with leeches who acquire their 'big guts' from sucking the blood from your legs and which you will extract by putting salt on them. For days on end the view will be nil and the rain will play a perpetual tattoo on the corrugated iron roof over your head. Meanwhile, the water will wash down from the heights above and the roar of minor landslides nearby and major landslides in the distance will be indistinguishable among the perpetual roar of thunder overhead. But soon the pleasant dry weather will return and the departing rain leaves a legacy of verdure and greenery, which enhances the charm of your hill station.

Enjoy your holiday.

CHAPTER 8
PEEP INTO PAKISTAN

In the days of the British 'Raj' (rule), India and Pakistan were one; there were areas in which Muslims predominated and areas in which Hindus were the majority. The reluctance of the Muslims, and their leader Jinnah in particular, to share independence with the Hindus brought about the partition of the country. The main Muslim areas are the north-west and north-east (excluding Assam), and these areas formed Pakistan. Economically, they were entirely dependent on the remainder of the sub-continent; the wheat of the Indus Basin supplied large areas, and their cotton was passed to the Hindu merchants and their mills.

In the eastern part, the cash crop jute was entirely processed in Calcutta and in the surrounding areas, which were outside Pakistan.

At the outset, then, the two parts of Pakistan were not economic units; nor were their Muslim inhabitants familiar with any skills other than in the realm of agriculture. The Hindus were the merchant and artisan classes, and they left for India. There is the oft-quoted example of the solitary Muslim trainee – an electrician – who was left to maintain the electricity supply to the whole of Lahore city, which is indicative of the plight of that new Commonwealth country. As soon as the country had time to breathe, the Kashmir conflict strained its resources to the utmost and diverted attention from the constitution-making process. The troubles associated with independence and the years 1947–9 also diverted attention from the inherent conflicts of the union of East and West Pakistan.

As the country developed its industrial potential, and as the initial difficulties were overcome, there were other problems to face. By far the greatest of these was the distance separating the two parts of Pakistan. It is, however, Mohammedanism, and that alone, which linked the two segments. Thus it can be understood that the differences in culture,

language, social and geographical characteristics and economic structure, which must be harmonised to secure a united Pakistan, are enormous. Underneath all political and constitutional wrangling this diversity
is uppermost, whether it be the allocation of development funds between
East and West, representation of both wings at the national level or allocation of posts in the civil service and the armed services. Thus it was that a
decision on when elections should take place was never taken. Moreover,
the terrific surge of communal feeling had scarcely died down sufficiently
for the problem of representation to be considered. Hence the formation of
non-communal political parties to contest elections proved a serious stum-
bling block to democratic development. The Muslim League, which was
the organisation that brought Pakistan into being, fell into disrepute and the
Awami League later followed suit. It has been said that the spirit of democracy is contrary to Muslim teaching, but however that may be, in 1957 a
coup d'état by senior army officers led to the overthrow of the Government
and a Martial Law Administration took its place.

The title of this chapter is not really justified, as I have never visited that
land of water – a veritable national Venice – which was East Pakistan. East and
West Pakistan finally separated; the East is a land which subsists only a few
feet above the waterways and delta of the two greatest of the sub-continent's
mighty rivers, the Ganges and Bramahputra. Yet East Pakistan was – with
due respect to West Pakistan – the more important portion of that bifurcated
country. For although East Pakistan was only one-sixth the size of the western
wing, it was not only the home of considerably more Pakistanis than the western wing – in all there were about 90 million Pakistanis – but its jute is probably the most important factor in the country's economy. Unfortunately, East
Pakistan is not so well known, for it has not the distinctiveness or the glamour
of a North West Frontier history to make films about. And although its people, being also Bengalis, are more politically minded, they strangely seldom
reach the highest levels in national leadership. Indeed, having left it to the West
Pakistanis to be the soldiers, they find that they have even less sway under the
Martial Law Administration.

So to West Pakistan we must turn our attention. And we find a land that could use the destructive water surplus of East Pakistan, for while the West's problem is water scarcity; the East's is floods. While both spend money on water control, the object in the West is to conserve as much as possible, and in the East to get rid of as much as possible. It is curious to observe that the sources of both the Indus River (the main provider of West Pakistan) and the Bramahputra (the main river of East Pakistan) are within a few miles of one another in western Tibet. If only the waters of the latter could be diverted westwards, what a difference it would make to both wings of the country!

The border of West Pakistan and India stretches for more than 1,500 miles – including the cease-fire line in Kashmir (although in its mountainous northern portion nobody knows where it is!). Along this enormous stretch there are but three legal points of transit between the two countries. There are two road crossings, one in the south near Hyderabad, the other at Ferozpur, and in addition, a road and rail transit point between Amritsar and Lahore. The crossing points are places of tourist interest and the Indian on holiday or business in Amritsar will pop down to the border to see the strange phenomenon. If he is over 30, he will recall the days when he and his pals used to nip into the lively life of Lahore for the evening – before partition. But in the last dozen years no more than a few hundred have done the 35-mile trip.

As you drive down from Amritsar to the frontier post at Attari, you recall that this is still the Grand Trunk Road which linked the erstwhile capital of British India – Calcutta – with the North West Frontier. But today it is a deserted road, and the railway track alongside boasts a solitary train a day in each direction and must be the least crowded of any of the sub-continent's trains. These fields have seen more deaths in recent years than probably any other area in the world, except perhaps Hiroshima. In the terrible times of 1947, Muslims, Hindus and Sikhs killed, and were killed, in their scores of thousands in this area. The appalling compulsion for destruction meant the loss of hundreds of thousands of lives in the Punjab and elsewhere.

But today all is peaceful. The border is demarcated by white posts down its whole length, but at Attari it is much more distinctive. You come across it unexpectedly amid the many brick-built villages, which are the most prosperous I've seen in India and whose land the Sikh owners till assiduously. The gate across the road is reminiscent of that of a level crossing; there are one or two tea-stalls, but also two sentries. And there is no railway line. I stop at the gate and wait for it to be opened. I wait in vain until I shout, "Koliye," and the sentry looks flabbergasted. In fact, only when he has again confirmed that someone incredibly wishes to go into Pakistan does he open the gate and direct me to the immigration shed. My formalities of form filling lasted a mere 45 minutes and customs clearance about two seconds – although they did inspect the tyres of my car so that they would know if I flogged them in Pakistan. I am told that it takes hours for a Pakistani to get into India and a corresponding length of time for an Indian to get into Pakistan. If they are unfortunate enough to travel by car, then they will find it still more difficult, as the car is almost taken to bits by Customs, and you can reassemble it yourself! They have good reason to be suspicious, for gold smuggling is a profitable enterprise in India. So profitable, indeed, that a recent diplomat imported an unofficial consignment in a secret compartment of his new car. The proceeds, in the form of Indian Rupee notes, he attempted to smuggle across to Lahore, but the Customs people, who were tipped off, held up the car for days until they finally found the secret compartment in the petrol tank. This gentleman now languishes in an Indian prison.

I had heard rumours in Amritsar that traffic in Pakistan had changed to the right-hand side of the road, so I enquired of the Indian Immigration officials. They just did not know, despite the fact that Pakistan was a mere 300 yards down the road – so much for the contacts maintained between both sides.

At last, off into no-man's land – which is tilled by a peasantry who may have been Indians or Pakistanis. And so past the horizontal red, white and green flag of India to the green and white with crescent moon and star of Pakistan, where the sentries were in grey and not a greenish khaki. I was shown to the Pakistan Immigration tent to be greeted by, "Did you hear the latest score?" I had not, but with glee I was told that the Pakistanis were almost an innings ahead of the West Indian cricket touring team, which had previously beaten the Indians. All ears were glued to the radio in the tent and I was later to see crowds gathered round the occasional radio at the tea stalls on the way into Lahore and in the city itself. It was just like the groups who assemble outside the TV shops at home for the cricket.

Pakistan is a different place; instead of the Mercedes-Benz trucks built in India and known as Tata-Mercedes, Pakistan had broken-down Bedfords and Dodges and Chevrolets; instead of tolerable roads, intolerable ones; the occasional bus even more decrepit than its Indian counterpart. The contrast was surprising – the villagers' homes were all of mud and there were virtually no brick dwellings to be seen until Lahore was reached. The villages reveal none of the 'middle-class' type – the occasional gent in Western-type clothes, who may be a schoolteacher or government official. Pakistan seemed devoid of them, and there were even fewer cycles than in India. The only feature to relieve all this is Batapur – the town of Bata shoes, manufactured in a modern factory quite out of place in this backward area. It is the most progressive manufacturing unit I have seen on the sub-continent, and its facilities are magnificent, providing housing, sports facilities and social services.

At the border one is informed by means of a great notice of the havoc wrought in 1947, so it is claimed, by the departing Sikhs and Hindus and the destruction by them to life and property. At the Shalimar Gardens in Lahore I was told that any defects which might be apparent are also due to the Sikhs – but in 1847, not 1947. This was when the great Sikh state of Ranjit Singh had its capital in Lahore – a time referred to by the Muslims of today as a period of 'occupation'. The Shalimar Gardens are beautiful nonetheless; they are Moghul gardens with typical ornamental ponds and wide grass verges. Surrounded by trees and descending by three or four levels, they present a vista of calm and beauty. And what is more, they were built by Muslims – true Pakistanis – which is something the Indians find difficult to explain away at the Taj Mahal (built during Muslim 'occupation', but by Hindu workmen, of course!).

The West Pakistan Assembly building in Lahore was unoccupied – apart from the sentries posted there by the Martial Law Administration – and the focus of government is now to be found in the cantonment, the whole area being known as Zone B. The Lahore cantonment presented a remarkable sight and would have gladdened the heart of any camp commandant of the British army. Almost every stone – moveable or fixed – was whitewashed, and even the curbs were painted; the immaculate state of every garden suggested that the corps d'élite of the Pakistan army must be a gardeners' battalion. This, however, is not so – the old-fashioned 'mali' is still at work, planting his grass by the blade rather than by the seed. And what a fine job he has done in between the notices directing one to military camp this, martial law office that, and don't turn left here, keep off the grass there, and the usual array of 'No Entry' signs. As is the wont of every army, each notice is in a galaxy of colours, which tend to confuse the eye, although psychologically no doubt they are of infinite value to the soldier. The roads are not only clean; they are sound.

They are probably the best roads to be found on the sub-continent in layout, surface and the number of roundabouts. The latter are not always an asset, for their size discourages cyclists who intend turning right from going all the way round them; hence you find yourself incessantly jamming on brakes to avoid a 'short-cutter'.

The city of Lahore is joined to the cantonment by the Mall – every cantonment has its mall, and that of Lahore is indeed impressive. It is lined by fine buildings, shops and parks and is wide enough to accommodate all users (bullock carts are specifically excluded by notices worded in English – it is a point for considerable thought whether the bullock cart owners can read English or whether it may be only English speakers who would drive bullock carts). But it is only one of the novelties one frequently encounters on one's travels, such as the alternate route avoiding floods labelled

'Driversion'; and there was that other road, apparently in a state of disre-
pair even before the water had began to lap over it, appropriately boasting
the warning 'Wavy Road'. I was to find, incidentally, that Pakistan traffic
was still on the left-hand side, because, I was informed on unsound authority, the bullocks refused to adopt such an Americanised procedure as using
the right-hand side of the road. Presumably they will wait for a new gener-
ation of bullocks to grow up!

One finds yet another mass of people in the old city of Lahore –
the populace is squeezed into an indecently small area and served by the
most frightful alleyways I have ever encountered. But they are quite clean.
Indeed, the streets of the bazaars amazed me with their absence of dirt.
Nobody had had the nerve to spit a single blood-red 'pan' onto the roadway since the Martial Law Administration took over. I was more scared to
drop a toffee paper in Lahore than to drop a fish and chip newspaper in the
centre of London – I think I would have been lynched by these public-spir-
ited Pakistanis.

Incidentally, I feel sure that the women of Lahore were very pretty,
although one had to go by two things. Firstly, the fact that the young school-
girls in Western rig or the Punjabi pyjamas (salwar kameez) and who were
not old enough to qualify for submergence in the burkhas (cloak) were very
attractive. Secondly, an occasional burkha revealed a neat pair of high-
heeled shoes and frequently a pretty ankle above them. It must be hot under
those things, but I suppose if our nuns can stand it, so can they. Indeed, the
anonymity of the burkha must have its blessings, and certainly some of the
ladies who disagreed with the shopkeepers would not have been so abu-
sive had they been face to face. But there are those who wear the sari, frequently with the end thrown over the right shoulder, thus distinguishing
them from their Hindu and Sikh brethren, who fling it over the left shoulder.
Nevertheless, the modern Pakistani woman in her salwar kameez is magnificent. Black hair, dark eyes, a tan which any Western girl would envy, a
tight-fitting shirt – and when I say tight I mean tight – and the loose white
trousers tied tightly at the ankles. I am told, on very good authority, that the

77

sleek fit of the shirt over waist and hips is enhanced by tying the trousers not around the waist, but rather in the position of the lower part of a bikini.

Pakistan was to be mine for one day only, so in good time to reach the border – closing time 7 p.m. – I bowled back along the road to Wagha to find it had been a busy day for the customs and immigration lads. Twenty-five persons had crossed on foot and five cars had passed through – it was time to rest after such a mass exodus mid-week. And what is more, it showed that the links which joined the two nations continued and that people were free to come and go as they pleased provided, of course, they could get a passport from one government, a visa from the other, a temporary resident's permit from the local authority, currency from a mysterious source and a strong constitution to brave the rigours of the crossing.

But there are two other ways – quite legal – of entering Pakistan from India, namely by air and by sea. In fact, the latter method is chosen by a Kashmiri friend of mine who lives ten miles from his brother – unfortunately, the latter resides on the other side of the cease-fire line. Undeterred by the paperwork and, what is more, successful at it, he leaves his home for Delhi (600 miles) then to Bombay (900 miles) then to Karachi by sea (600 miles) to Lahore (800 miles), and to his brother's home from there it is a mere 170 miles. He is, as you will gather, very fond of his brother. But that is not all; he is a trader in the trinkets and local handicrafts line, and his brother is a salesman to tourists in his part of the world. Such goods do the journey to Bombay, but from there they go to Bahrain in the Persian Gulf and then are transhipped to Karachi. I am uncertain as to the reason for this, but perhaps it is merely a reflection of the wanderlust which has gripped this particular family...

Karachi has been the capital of Pakistan and now, much to the annoyance of traders and shop keepers, the Government is moving to a brand new site a thousand miles away in the foothills of the Himalayas, which when built will be known as Islamabad. Karachi is a town on its own. It receives all the imports for the western wing, but as there is little but desert for hundreds of miles around, Karachi extracts its needs and the remainder is shifted up country to the Lahore-Rawalpindi-Peshawar area, where live most of West Pakistan's population. Karachi has expanded from 350,000 people at independence to 2,000,000 in 12 years – what other city can boast such a record of expansion? There has, however, been little expansion of facilities to cope with such an appalling influx of refugees. They came, of course, from India at partition, and thus are mostly newcomers to the country without any great attachment to Karachi. Some would like to return to India where they have relatives, but cannot do so, for they are now Pakistani citizens. Others will follow trade and work to the new capital in the north. Karachi is not the place one could feel any great attachment for; it is on the fringe of the desert and sea and gets the worst of both worlds. There is not enough water and there is too much sand. Everything has been makeshift, for Karachi was never intended as a capital city. From government, and government buildings, to accommodation and transport, everything is or has been temporary. But the town is clean and there is a considerable awareness of traffic regulations. Woe betide he who crosses anywhere but at the pedestrian crossing. The burkha is not so much in evidence as in Lahore.

Poor Pakistan; it is desperately poor, so makeshift, so incoherent a national entity. Most nations – even the poorest and smallest – make a show of their government buildings, a president's palace or national museum or ceremonial parade ground. Something, in fact, which they can justifiably put in their guidebooks and tourist handouts to merit a visit. Karachi has nothing and its National Museum evokes a sense of pity and despair. It is located in quite a small and out-of-the way building and indicates little of the past or present of Pakistan, apart from some relics of the old Indus Basin city of Mohenjo-Daro. It is not only the poverty of the people but an organised unified existence that is lacking. But the effort is being made. Some might deplore the standards evident at, for example, the Pakistan Industrial Fair, but it is a start and a start in the right direction. The textile products of the country are improving rapidly; plastics are now produced in Pakistan, and although the railway coaches may have been manufactured in Germany and the lorries imported, nevertheless Ford is now assembling cars at Karachi. In due course a well-balanced industrial potential should emerge to give employment, reduce the country's dependence upon imports, modify the reliance upon agriculture and ultimately raise the standard of living.

CHAPTER 9
INDEPENDENT NEPAL

Nepal – how did it get there? Why is it not a part of Tibet or of India? How did the eight million Nepalese gain their independence? The answer is that they didn't. They have always been independent and have never been part of anyone's empire. And the reason is not far to seek – remember the Gurkhas? When the innumerable Indian states were being absorbed into the Indian Empire, the friendly Himalayas, plus the Gurkhas in their far-flung kingdom, fought to retain their independence, and the treaty signed in 1814 between Britain and Nepal guaranteed that each would respect the sovereignty of the other.

If you want to go there you have two choices of route – by air from India or overland from the plains along the newly built 'highway', which, however, is limited to a single track and has not been metalled. It is, in short, unwise to trust your car to this road, which stretches 90 miles in order to accomplish what the crow can do in 13. But make no mistake about it; the days when diplomatic mail entered by pony carriers is only a year or two gone, for during the monsoon, planes frequently found it impossible to land on the precarious airstrip of Kathmandu. If you can disguise yourself as merchandise, you can choose an alternative route by train to the railhead, which is a few miles inside Nepal territory, and then by ropeway – on the principle of a ski lift, but quite unlike one – over the mountains and down into the valley. But I wouldn't risk it – it is in an appalling state of disre-pair, and the supporting pylons are thick with rust. Nevertheless, the bulk of goods entering the Kathmandu valley travel by this means – rice, wheat, cement, whatever.

But let us face up to it – the traveller of today uses today's inventions – and we travel into Kathmandu by plane. At Patna, in the heart of India, one is confronted with the fact that one is leaving India. It is rather like being asked for your passport in the Hebrides. But it is true – at Patna, Indian and Nepalese officials check visas, baggage and people. You are issued with forms to complete – and the Englishman's first reaction is that there is some mistake; the form is headed 'On His Majesty's Service'; surely it should be 'On *Her* Majesty's Service'. Sorry, come back to the Himalayas – you are about to complete a form for the benefit of the Government of the Kingdom of Nepal.

Whilst the almost deserted airfield throbs in the heat, you drink cold Coca-Colas in the lounge shared with the third Prince of Nepal, who, accompanied by an American lady friend, is on his way to the States via Calcutta. His personal plane is being refuelled for the onward journey.

Later, in the sky, the impenetrable wall of ice stretching from Annapurna on the left and Kanchenjunga to the right makes one ask in desperation, "Where is Nepal and little Kathmandu?" The jungle of the Terai gives way to green mountains, which surround the valley of Kathmandu. But valley is a misnomer – a valley implies an opening at either end, but Kathmandu is in a 'bowl' completely surrounded by mountains four to five thousand feet above the city itself. As the bowl is only about 15 to 20 miles in diameter, the airmen amongst you will realise some of the difficulties in landing. But that is not all – the Kathmandu 'bowl' is a mass of small plateaux between which the earth appears to have been scooped out. The airport was built on the biggest and best of these, but as it was not long enough, a bit has been added and the 'ends' of the plateau have been shored up by concrete. The finished product more closely resembles an aircraft carrier – if you overshoot, down you go, and you haven't got the advantage of the aircraft carrier's manoeuvrability; if the wind is in the wrong direction, you still have to chance it or go back to Patna. There are a number of examples of those that should have returned to Patna – instead, the wrecks lie below the incoming pilot as a reminder and as an incentive to come again tomorrow.

Envisage a capital city – roads coming in from all directions entering the heart of the great town, bustling with traffic, ill-tempered pedestrians fighting to cross the roads through the traffic jams; cars, people, noise, petrol fumes, more people, more cars, more buildings. Now forget the vision, for this is the capital city of Kathmandu, where the 'roads' peter out long before they get anywhere, for there is nowhere for them to go. And pursuing this logic, is there, therefore, any purpose in having them paved? Of course not, although one or two concessions are made to modify various sections. And so we find that the road to the embassies of Britain and India, to the King's Palace and the Prime Minister's residence, and linking the centre of town are metalled. The road to the airport at one time knew this form of construction, but I would have preferred a dust-track road. The airport road had both and it is the contrast that hurts – six feet of 'good' road is followed by two feet of bad!

You do not choose your hotel; you decide if you are American or British and then the problem resolves itself. To the Royal Hotel for the former, to the Snow View for the latter. I must add that there are certain exceptions to this, but this is the pattern.

To the awed traveller, the Snow View is much more then he expected. There he finds that electricity is available for lighting and he tentatively toys with the idea of using his electric razor after all. Having nearly electrocuted himself – the voltage being 110 – he is then told that there is a power cut and that electricity is rationed anyway. It is a brave man who watches the blades of his razor stagger round rather than at the maker's guarantee of umpteen revolutions per second! All 'mod cons', did you say? Of course, the proprietor's wife is a Canadian who understands the delicacies of the Western way of life. Furthermore, they cater for most of the parties of Himalayan climbers. I am led into a room with a toilet, which is, of course, the Eastern floor squat and get cramp type – but with a difference. A thunderbox has been placed on the top for the convenience of Western guests.

Kathmandu is not Nepal. It is a failing with many Londoners that they regard their city as being England, and the good citizens of Kathmandu are inclined to think in this manner also. And they have a much greater reason for regarding the valley as Nepal. Communications with other parts of the country are, to put it mildly, poor. Of course, the Royal Nepalese Airlines run services to other centres; that is, a solitary Dakota flogs itself to death providing a once or twice a week service to three towns in other parts of Nepal, which boast still more precarious landing strips. Then there are communications of a sort overland. Tibetans and country folk walk many miles over trackless wastes to bring produce to the market at Kathmandu. From afar, perhaps 200 miles away, handicrafts, beaten brass ornaments and the like are brought on the backs of coolies; from the sides of the Kathmandu 'bowl', firewood is carried by porters, who sell it mainly at the burial places for cremations – the burning ghats on the little river. The half a million souls in the valley then regard themselves as Nepal. If they want to visit another part of the country, they must go into India and then again into Nepalese territory, such is the lack of communications. There are two British recruiting stations for Gurkhas in Nepal, at which preliminary training is done before the recruits leave. They are at the extreme ends of Nepal, 600 miles apart. But one has to undertake a most tedious three-day journey – most of it in Indian territory – to get from either of them to Kathmandu. In some parts of Nepal only Indian currency is, in practice, acceptable, such is the isolation of these areas.

The tourist books inform one that there are three cities in the valley – Batgaon, Patan (not to be confused with Patna) and Kathmandu. That is true, but I would like to mention a further one, or rather to split Kathmandu between the visitors' city and the old. The visitors' city is largely that of the Americans; there are almost 60 families there, working mainly for US aid missions, with accommodation on quite a lavish scale, most of it new. There are also about 30 Britons, some of whom are at the embassy. Most of the other foreigners are Indian. But the old city – that of the Nepalese – is in chronic need of sanitation. One gets the impression that the Nepalese have potentially more wealth to develop than the Indians, and their need is education rather than capital. If someone were to donate a few hundred tons of DDT to Kathmandu it would be a boon.

As I entered one street, with its mud and brick dwellings – with the sewage running in streams on either side – the flags were flying. My Englishorientated mind immediately jumped to the brilliant conclusion that a carnival was in the offing. The gay bunting of all colours stretched across the street from house to house the full length of the road. It was clearly a big effort and I wondered if this was perhaps the Nepalese 'Christmas'. I was later disillusioned: cholera had struck and the lines of flags were designed to trip up the evil cholera spirits as they come in to land to attack their next victim. However, oblivious of this at the time, and in the true spirit of 'fools walk in', I did just this at the invitation of a 'shopkeeper' to his home – barefooted, of course. His home, that of a relatively well-to-do small 'entrepreneur', was on two floors. On the ground floor were two tiny rooms, one of which was a kitchen. The floors, walls and ceilings appeared to be of mud and mud only, so it was with some trepidation that I climbed up the rickety wooden steps to the 'first floor'. It was not far to go, for the ceilings were less than six feet from the floor. Upstairs, again all mud. There was no closely defined right angle between wall and floor, but instead uncertainty as to where one ended and the other began, for the room was almost a hollow scooped from the walls. Of wardrobes, dressing tables, and even beds, there were none. There would be no room for the latter, and even had there been, to sit up in bed would have meant a violent altercation with the ceiling. Mats, I should add, serve the purpose of our foam mattresses. During my visit the floor did not cave in and there were no serious accidents, despite the gloom, for the window apertures are permanently blocked during the cold of winter. Glass is much too expensive a commodity – it is only the very biggest and best that can afford to have windowpanes flown in from the outside world. This, incidentally, gave rise in part to a feature of Nepal that is greatly admired today. On many older buildings – even those which might now be described as tenements – the wooden shutters in place of windows are exquisitely carved, and these decorative windows are to be found everywhere. They are opened in summertime and closed in winter, but their profusion gives Kathmandu much of its charm.

On the subject of housing, it behoves us to visit the King's Palace, which could be described as a bigger and more ornate Buckingham Palace.

Kathmandu must boast more lavish buildings per head of the population than any other city in the world. Nepal has not yet reached that stage of 'progress' where the creations of the past must have their historic purpose destroyed in order to serve the needs of the present. Palaces then have not yet become government offices. But perhaps in Nepal this has been taken to extremes, for the King no longer lives in his palace. Instead, he has built himself a neat 'little' wooden modern villa by the side of the old, and the palace remains empty. But this may not be for long, for a new democratic regime and Parliament and Government are now looking for somewhere to meet ... So, no doubt, the Belgravia of Kathmandu will follow suit and become a haven of government and commercial offices; embassies and institutions and the wealthy citizens will move further into the 'bowl' and buy a suburban plateau for themselves.

The main export of Nepal is the Gurkhas. Tourism is beginning to compete, but the famous soldiers of two world wars are still in demand not only in the British army but in the Indian army also. The Indian army is every bit as proud of its Gurkhas as the British army. And, of course, there is yet another army that calls for the fighting spirit of the Gurkha – the Nepalese army itself. The visitor, or indeed any observer of Nepal, is inevitably inclined to expect a degree of backwardness in the country. But this cannot be said of the army; their officers and men are impeccable in uniform and turnout; their military displays on Asia's greatest parade ground – the Tundikhal – are a lesson to many nations of the west in smartness and discipline. But, you may ask, why the enormous expenditure on an army? Where is the danger? After all, the Chinese can hardly attack, and the Pakistanis have no common frontier. The answer, until recently, was the fear of India to the south, and there was a strong body of feeling in Nepal that any acceptances of military or economic assistance from that quarter were suspect. Nepal is, in some respects, to India what Ireland is to Britain. The Nepalese may go to India and get jobs in much the same way as the Irish can find work in England without nationality problems arising.

But to return to the army: their military areas are bedecked with notices discouraging stopping to gaze; no day passes without some part of Kahtmandu being mixed up in military manoeuvres, and one is given the impression that every man over 18 in the country has been given his call-ing-up papers to cope with an impending emergency. We have all heard of the kukri, and if you haven't, certainly the Communists in Malaya's jun-gles have learnt to fear the knives of the Gurkhas as they stalked their prey through the jungle in a way no English soldier could. Their army is not well equipped with heavy material, but one would not expect it to be. They are saved the embarrassment of a navy, air force and marines, and so there is no problem of the various fighting services fighting for funds between each other – the army is first, second and last, and it gets full support from the people. But this is not to say that the Nepalese are without their problems. Lurking just beneath the surface they have a minor racial problem on their minds, for the Gurkhas in 1768 were the invaders of Nepal, coming from more remote parts and defeating the Newaris, a race more Aryan and less Mongol in features. Today, both groups call themselves Nepalese and it is to be hoped that the relative amity of recent years between them will be main-tained to give Nepal an opportunity of making progress in the betterment of the lives of its people, regardless of origin.

Who can speak of Nepal without mentioning the mysterious stupas (stone temples) and the five-tiered pagodas? Who can forget the incredi-ble square at Patan, which is full of these pagodas and shrines? And not only are they to be found in the towns, but in the countryside also. They are, in fact, towns in themselves, these sites of stupas, such as that of Bodhnath. This is a Buddhist shrine of considerable note; it lies in a tiny oasis of Tibetan territory and the King of Nepal exercises no authority over the representative of the Dalai Lama – the Chinia Lama – who is the Dalai Lama's 'archbishop' in Nepal. He is a very pleasant individual, keen to share his whisky and proud of his knowledge of English, which he learnt in India. He lives in no way an ascetic life with his wife and children, and the floor of his home is covered by magnificent carpets and the walls are draped

– over draped – with prayer mats, ornaments and pictures. His establishment has an enormous stupa with the mysterious eye staring from the golden top of the building. The establishment also boasts a jeep, which in the complete absence of any bus service does the three- or four-mile trip into Kathmandu to get the more refined requirements to keep the organisation going. In short, the wealth of Bodhnath is an example to the rest of the valley to pull its socks up and aspire to greater things – in this world and the next.

The Nepalese are very religious, or perhaps it is that a certain propor-tion, prominent to the onlooker, is over-zealous. Be that as it may, the visi-tor cannot but fail to be impressed by the devout, who will kiss the spot on which a monkey has just perched. It may be unhygienic, but it is frequently done, especially near the temples where the abundance of monkeys pro-vides every opportunity to the faithful.

It is usual for the dead to be cremated in Nepal and the burning ghats by the river's edge are for this purpose. When the body has been consumed by fire, the ashes are thrown into the stream. These are the simple facts, but the west has no monopoly in the field of time and motion study. The Nepalese have calculated the time and energy involved in bringing the dead down to the ghats; it is much better if they can get the decrepit down while they still have a little of their own steam left for the journey. It does not fol-low that a Nepalese old age pension means a place at the burning ghat, but the proximity of the ghats gives inspiration to the sick to get well soon, or else... A thoughtful municipality has converted an old palace nearby for the relief of the infirm, and so a large proportion of the sick come here to get well in the shade of the temples, and if they don't, well, private enterprise has ensured that they shall not want in their last earthly need. The wood merchants come into their own; in fact, you can't help tripping over their bundles at every step, for the dead at Pashupatinath are big business. Like all societies, there is a division of class: there is one ghat, or place, reserved just for the King when he dies and his ashes are thrown into the river.

The Nepalese are a people headed for the 20th century who are just beginning to absorb the first 'benefits' of Western civilisation. The women in their saris, the men in their tight trousers and the children who suffer so greatly from elephantitis – that ghastly swelling of the limbs, which in its initial stages gives a 'bonny baby' impression – will all begin to demand more than their tiny rice field and will call for an improvement in their appallingly low standard of living. But some are on the way up – the bicycle has proved wondrously popular and the dishevelled policeman on point duty makes sure that they have their lights on after dark. Indeed, when I wished to hire a cycle on my first evening I was told that as a light wasn't available it couldn't be done. Undaunted, I said that the legal technicality did not trouble me, but they were horrified and indicated that I would be acquiring accommodation at an address other than the Snow View Hotel.

One has to leave eventually and my excuse to prolong my stay was over. From the Snow View Hotel I passed the Surrey country house, set in its own gardens, which does duty as the British Embassy. I was driven by taxi jeep back to the airport and to the Indian Airlines Corporation Dakota, with its beautiful hostess. Apart from one or two Indians bemoaning the inefficiency of the Nepalese officials – "It wouldn't be done like this in India" – we boarded the plane and were soon climbing high between and then over the mountains, back to the intense heat of India's plains.

CHAPTER 10
THE RULERS

Please bear with me, but if this chapter is too technical, skip to Chapter 11.

In 1935, a new Constitution was implemented, which created the federal structure of India; the Cripps mission of 1942 was followed by the Labour Cabinet mission of 1946 to investigate the means whereby India could gain her independence inside or outside the Commonwealth.

Lord Wavell, as Governor-General, had held elections in late 1945 for the Provincial Assemblies, at which about 25% of the adult population had the vote. The Congress Party led with the Muslim League gaining about a quarter of the number of votes of Congress. The visiting mission proposed a three-tier structure: a central body, responsible only for foreign affairs, defence and communications, with the provinces and princely states responsible for all other functions. The third element was to be a voluntary grouping of provinces and states by mutual agreement. This set-up was to continue for ten years, after which time the structure was to be reviewed.

The motivation of this policy, and indeed the constitutional development of the sub-continent, revolved round the Hindu–Muslim problem. The one feared the other, and as the Muslims were in a minority, they were very unhappy about their position in an independent India. Although the mission's proposals might have solved the problem, the antagonism between the two communities was too great to be tempered by rational thinking. The two creeds could not come to terms, although at one stage both sides did agree to take part in an interim government.

The Cabinet mission failed; Lord Wavell was replaced by Lord Mountbatten, and a further attempt was made to resolve fears and difficulties. This time, two Constituent Assemblies were to be formed, thus acknowledging the 'Two-Nation' theory. But the aim was a united India, perhaps postponed ten years, but nevertheless attainable if both Hindus and Muslims should wish it.

The terms for the Constituent Assemblies were based upon one representative per million inhabitants. In the provinces, the Muslim League and Congress members of the Assemblies were to elect their representatives on this basis. There were two qualifications with regard to Punjab and Bengal, and in these two areas either community could declare for partition of their provinces. Both voted in favour of partition and a boundary commission divided both Punjab and Bengal. In the event, 291 Hindus were elected and sat in the Constituent Assembly in New Delhi, whilst 80 Muslims formed the Pakistan Constituent Assembly to sit at Karachi.

In this way, the great sub-continent attained its independence, but was divided into three parts – India, East Pakistan and West Pakistan. In retrospect, the communal troubles that accompanied independence were of such intensity as to suggest that continued unity would not have created any greater disruption and destruction. At the same time, the unity of the sub-continent would have been preserved, but whether to the greater benefit of all its people or not will never be known.

By 1951, the new Indian Constitution had been argued about, compromised on and finally promulgated. Under its terms, India is a Federal, Parliamentary democracy, in which the reserve of power is held by the Central Authority – that is, only certain specified powers are in the hands of the state Governments. There is a two-chamber legislature at the centre, with a president who acts upon the advice of his ministers, who are members of the majority party in the Lok Sabha (Lower House). The Lower House is elected by single-member constituencies on the basis of universal suffrage. The Judiciary is independent and the Constitution provides for the American concept of judicial review of legislation to ensure that nothing in Acts of Parliament is contrary to the Constitution. Furthermore, the president may ask the Judiciary for an opinion on any aspect of the Constitution which is open to more than one interpretation.

Thus in some respects the Indian Constitution resembles that of the United States – its federal structure, judicial review and the requirement of something more than a simple majority for amendment of the Constitution. In India, amendment requires a vote of two-thirds of both Houses, with a minimum of 50% of membership.

The Cabinet system is perhaps the most outstanding feature, and the doctrines of ministerial and collective responsibility are observed. The procedures and terms used in the House of the People (Lower House) and the Council of States (Upper House) are remarkable in their resemblance to our own; the 'Estimates', 'Civil Contingencies Fund', 'Table of the House' and many others are all terms used in India also.

The 16 federal states of India are based mainly on the linguistic divisions throughout the country. These 16 take the place of the multitude of princely states – which numbered nearly 600 – plus the old provinces of British India. There are few exceptions to the 16: a few centrally administered and backward areas, such as mountain-locked Tripura and Manipur in the east, Himachal Pradesh, which is inhabited by mountain peoples reluctant to be absorbed into the Punjab, some islands off the coast, plus the federal territory of Delhi. To achieve such a coherent structure, the rights of many suffered, but a degree of arbitrariness was inevitable when such a chaotic jumble of administrative units was presented to the first independent Indian Government. Clearly, many of the frictions aggravate the political scene from time to time. The Nagas in their mountain jungles and the Sikhs in strategic Punjab vie with each other for newspaper prominence from time to time. The bifurcation of Bombay state has brought political satisfaction to the Mahratti and Gujerati linguistic groups, but aggravated a number of good souls in the region of Nagpur, who want yet another state carved out of three to form Vidarba and protect their interests, which they feel are neglected by their lack of unity.

The degree of independence at state level is not so strong. A year or two ago, the Chief Minister of the Punjab was having his troubles and the loyalties of the members of the Legislature were uncertain. He thus did not wish to jeopardise his position by asking for a vote of confidence. Nonetheless, the party headquarters in Delhi directed him to seek such a vote, regardless of the outcome, and this he was obliged to do. This instance, however, attained considerable publicity because it was so unusual.

The role of the president is similar to that of the monarch in Britain. The Indian Constitution stipulates that all actions of the Government are done in the name of the president; thus there is ample scope for an irresponsible man to act arbitrarily and not on the advice of his ministers, as the Queen, by convention, does in Britain. In practice, however, President Prasad has acted in the best traditions and maintains his prestige as a figurehead and not as an interventionist in affairs of state. Impartiality is meticulously maintained. Of course, were a president to intervene, he would do so at the risk of jeopardising his chances of re-election at the end of his five-year term of office. By convention, if the president is from north India, then the vice-president is from the south.

In looking for signs of weakness and strength in Indian democracy, we must also look inside the Parliament building, at the proceedings and how they are conducted. In the semi-circular House of the People we find the Speaker, somewhat less formal and more jovial than in the House of Commons, but maintaining a balance between Government and Opposition speakers. Perhaps one may hear a long speech criticising the Government's English language policy by Opposition member Mr Frank Anthony representing the Anglo-Indian viewpoint, while Mr Nehru listens attentively. On the other hand, Question Time will bring forth enquiries about why trains in the hon. gentleman's constituency are always late, or why a maternity clinic has not been opened.

Let us hope that India's economic development will be sufficiently rapid that its people may not become dissatisfied with all forms of democratic rule, the traditions and practices of which have been carefully nurtured since Independence.

CHAPTER 11
THE RULED

We are familiar with very little of India's life, for no newspapermen take photographs of the beautiful Parsee girls on Juhu Beach, Bombay, nor have we heard of Calcutta's Chowringhee, and the odd photo of the sari-clad air hostess does little to inform the world about the sexy salwar kameez (tight-fitting shirt with trousers) of the Delhi University girls.

This India, however, is very real; this country, though no larger than Arabia and only one-third the size of the United States, is the home of twice the population of the whole of Africa. Four hundred and twenty millions are crowded into this land, which presents a degree of homogeneity that is unsurpassed elsewhere. For where else would you get a population so united – by religion, by race, by colour, by economic activity and a similar climate? Indeed, even in language the homogeneity is apparent. In religion, they are primarily Hindu, for the dissident element in their society – the Muslims – were largely expelled at the time of partition, and the Muslim minority – 40 millions – have curiously become more Indian than the Indians themselves. Thus it is in Uttar Pradesh, which has a very large Muslim population, where the advocacy of Hindi as a national language is strongest. In fact, there is scarcely even a Protestant-Catholic-type problem, for the Protestants of Hinduism, the Sikhs, number no more than ten million. There are, inevitably in such a large country, minor communities, such as Parsees and Christians. Thus Hinduism, the religion and way of life, unifies the nation to a degree that would have been impossible in an undivided India.

With regard to race and colour, it need only be said that the further south one goes, the darker is the complexion, but this is a matter of degree only. It should be said, however, that any secession movements that do exist are comparable only to those of the Welsh or Scottish Nationalists and to be found mainly in the south. It is here that one gets the sharpest distinctions between the so-called Dravidian races and the Aryan races of the north. But even in such areas, the numbers speaking Hindi are increasing, and in any event, the people of Rajasthan and Punjab can understand those from Bengal, for Hindi, Punjabi and Bengali are akin to one another. The comparison is between Spanish and Portuguese, for the people of both of these countries can usually understand the speech of the other.

The economic activity which links the peoples is agriculture, for it is practised by similar methods throughout the land; the only difference being that some areas cultivate predominantly rice in preference to wheat. The climate is happily described as hot – the Himalayas being an obvious exception and the desert areas having less rain than others. Like all generalisations, we can now delight in picking holes in the above – the Nagas appear to be most anxious to have an independent state of their own; the Sikhs are clamouring for something similar; the Kashmiris we don't know about, although it is probable that many, especially those connected with the tourist trade, would now opt to remain with India. Nonetheless, a remarkable homogeneity exists throughout the land, despite all remarks to the contrary. A very distinct Indian nationalism is to be felt in all communities, although it is perhaps amongst the Sikhs that the greatest degree of superciliousness exists. For many feel a quiet satisfaction at the preponderance of Sikhs in high places in the armed forces, and they point out that no Hindu has yet been Army Chief of Staff and that the non-bearded gentlemen in that post have been from the small warrior race of Coorgis in south India.

The democratic nature of Hinduism contributes to the success of democracy in India's political life. Hinduism, unlike the dogma of Christianity, accepts all religions as a part of the whole religion of mankind; as a Christian you are in fact a Hindu, so there is no question of your conversion to Hinduism. To the man in the street, Communism is associated with Christianity, for it was the Christian-majority Kerala that once elected a Communist government in that state!

The Indian woman has been regarded as being subservient and downtrodden. However, it is in India that we have seen a woman at the head of the country's foremost political party, the Congress, and a woman in one of the chief diplomatic posts, as High Commissioner to Britain! No, the allegation about Indian women is not true, and I am confident that there are just as many hen-pecked Indian husbands as there are English ones – in a proportion of eight to one, of course.

And now we will take a look at another facet of life - marriage. The classical view is that westerners marry whom they love; the Indian loves whom they marry. Idealistic but hardly accurate. Basically, the Indian conception of marriage sees it as another stage of life; one no more chooses one's partner in marriage than one's brothers and sisters. Thus, as the individual is presented with a brother or sister, so one is presented with wife or husband. In any event, the proceedings were undertaken at an early age, and teenagers were merely presented with a fait accompli, which was henceforth a part of their lives. The introduction of Western influences is playing havoc with the old system, and child marriages (which were usually not consummated immediately) are forbidden by law. In Bengal, the marrying age among the educated is rising rapidly, and girls may still be unmarried in their twenties. There may be a suitable match, but there are many cases where an offer has been turned down by the parents precisely because they suspected it of being something of a love match! Moreover, as one Indian Air Force flight lieutenant told me, who expected to marry shortly, but not to the girl he would like: "My father would not object, but whilst my experience is limited, and may prove false after marriage, he has chosen successfully for my two elder brothers."

But let's face it, the contract is a forced one, and many couples today feel no obligation of loyalty to their partner and continue their affairs after marriage with no sense of guilt. Their viewpoint is that they were pushed into it; they could no more think of going against their parents' wishes than sprouting wings. But the technicality of marriage did not affect their own feelings, intentions and actions. Those that get their own way do not always make a success of it, and there are probably just as many failures as in the West. The lass who finds a lad to marry for love and not for the dowry he can pocket says, "I'm glad you love me for myself, and not for what you can get out of me."

The arranged marriage is still prevalent, but in the educated home an element of democracy can be discerned. So let us have a peep into the home of Surinder, a pretty 18-year-old lass who has decided against going on to university and has declared, "I want to get married." As a westerner you will immediately enquire, "To whom?" But her statement is one of intent only, and the specific gentleman has not yet been 'earmarked'. Her statement merely means that the search must begin, and Dad must check his bank balance to see into what social class he can expect to 'buy' her with a dowry he can afford. Now, I am unable to indicate a government scale of rates – for the amount of the dowry depends not only on whether she marries a diplomat (which, incidentally, is one of the pluses), an army officer, a shopkeeper or a junior clerk (while right down at the bottom of the social structure, the Untouchable reverses the procedure and pays the girl!), but also how beautiful, intelligent, how light-skinned and how old she is. All will play a part, and as Surinder's dad is a middle-level civil servant, an army officer – captains are popular and fairly young – is thought to be just about right.

But there is no army cantonment nearby, so off she is packed to relatives in Deolali near Bombay, where her uncle is a colonel. Being a liberal family, a sort of debutante series is inaugurated, taking the form of parties and dances, and Surinder surveys the lads while the colonel surveys the parents of the lads. A shortlist is easily made, and negotiations, which involve more subtleties than a summit conference, ensue. A popular method once preliminary negotiations have taken place is to stage a tea party. When all have drunk tea, everybody knows the drill and they find that it is time to go, eventually leaving the prospective bride and groom on their own. It is at this stage that the hidden microphone and television camera get a bigger story than they would at the opening of Parliament. In this country – I am told – it is handy to break the ice with a suggestion that a drink might be desired. In hottest India, this is likewise a good icebreaker, despite the fact that they've been knocking back tea for an hour. But it is at the arm round the shoulder, lips to cheek stage that variations appear. By this time, our Indian male has probably discussed the weather, indicated his pay and prospects and is declaring: "I have to get married some time, and you appear to be a girl I would like to marry and be the mother of my children. May our parents get together and talk the matter over seriously and in detail? Mind you, I would be prepared to accept a dowry of Rs 10,000." (£800 and twice as much as Surinder's pop had in mind.)

And so the romantic mood reaches its climax. If the girl is more westernised than he, our army captain is in for a rebuff, and it is convenient for her to express surprise as to his intentions – and at an innocent tea party too! But there we are – a pretty girl will not want for suitors, and in the land of India a lass or lad of more than marriageable age will be the despair of their parents – the girl's father will go about increasing the dowry offered, and the lad's father will advertise that he will accept a smaller dowry and, what is more, consider a dark-complexioned girl.

And so, eventually, the marriage will take place, without any marriage certificate, in a series of ceremonies described very fully in many other books. So suffice it then to wish them a happy married life, provided we can make ourselves heard through the din of raucous bands playing 'Colonel Bogey' and 'Tea for Two'.

The choice of tunes does not reflect their disregard for religious occasions – although many Indians are just as good agnostics as many of us are. But let us follow this joyous couple in their married life; he will come home and complain about the amount of work he has to do and about how he would like to be in the Money Earning Service – sorry, Military Equipment Supplies Branch – rather than in the Artillery. They will complain about the servants, saying that they are useless and will have to go.

They enjoy their 'Christmas', Dussehra in October and Divali in November, when lights are lit everywhere and presents of sweets exchanged, but these are rituals with not such a spiritual meaning for them as in former days. They will visit the temple only on special occasions. Of their religious festivals, Divali is perhaps the most important, and in contrast to our big festival which celebrates a birth, that of the pacific Hindu commemorates a fight. At Holi in spring there is the festival at which coloured dyes are flung at one and all, and it is advisable to wear one's oldest clothes, for Europeans as well as Indians come in for a share of the proceeds. But the coming of the monsoon, though not an official festival, is one of the most joyous, for it means the end of the insufferable heat of summer, and their children will come out into the streets without clothes to let the wondrous rains of the first downpours soak into their skins.

I think most westerners have heard something about caste and the Untouchables. Certain opinions have it that a section of the population of India suffers the rigours of something worse than a colour bar and is depressed, downtrodden and desperately poor. No doubt various tales have seeped through about the upper-class Indian who demands that these good souls do not permit their shadows to fall on him; that if he is accidentally touched by a Harijan (Untouchable), he will jump into the first train and dash home to change his clothes – after he has cursed the poor Untouchable in no uncertain manner.

I must inform you that these tales are very wide of the mark – in the India of today. Moreover, you have heard of such stories because they are news – they would be headline news in much the same way as the juicy cases are here. In the dim and distant past of India's history, someone clearly had the idea that dirt pollutes and is a danger to health. But they did not have the medical know-how to combat the diseases which spring from dirt, hence those whose unfortunate job it was to keep the place clean were segregated and their employers would have nothing to do with them. Over the years, this arrangement became so established that it evolved as a virtual tenet of the Hindu faith. It is, of course, nothing of the kind, although one will still find areas in which caste distinctions are regarded as such.

The task of eliminating this discrimination has been a long and arduous one. The Harijans, as they are known today, have a long history of suppression, and from this downtrodden state they are learning to rise. The Government are doing all they can to help these people – they are allocated a certain number of places in the Civil Service and they are designated as a special community with certain advantages in the Indian constitution. Indeed, discrimination against them is an offence.

Vegetables heading for Simla.

Village water carriers. Rajasthan.

Baby transport in the hills. Mussoorie.

Henley maybe; but Kashmir, not the Thames.

A Shikara, the Kashmiri gondola.

Economy train travel. Bengal.

Preferred transport, Hooghly River, Calcutta.

CHAPTER 12
REFUGEES

In recent years, the world has heard a great deal about refugees; there have been so many coming from and going to so many places and for many different reasons. These people have been white-complexioned, brown, black and yellow. In India, when one speaks of refugees one is referring to the people involved in the exchange of population, for it was no less than that at the time of independence and partition and, to a lesser extent, ever since.

Estimates of the numbers involved vary, but it is clear that many millions migrated. Millions of Muslims went to Pakistan, mainly from the eastern Punjab, Delhi, Uttar Pradesh, Bihar and West Bengal. In exchange, virtually every Hindu, and certainly every Sikh, migrated from West Pakistan into India, and there was a huge exodus of Hindus from East Pakistan to West Bengal. Thus, throughout northern India, an amazing 'general post' took place, involving – some observers estimate – 40 million people. The 'exchange' was marked by the most appalling riots and killings – doubtful stories circulate as to which side started it. Whatever the causes, today the resettlement of refugees is still a major problem, although with regard to India, the influx from West Pakistan has benefited the country's economy.

The Sikhs (and the Punjabis generally), with their reputation for hard work, for their capacity to get the best from a poor soil, form a very considerable community in the northern parts. It is remarkable that enquiries as to where one comes from will so frequently elicit the reply, "What is now Pakistan." The Sikhs held much land in the irrigated areas of the Punjab, in the Indus–Chenab–Jhelum River regions, and on leaving for India they, like the other refugees, lost the lot. The lack of bitterness is amazing and the resilience with which they have met the blow is heartening. One family, which possessed many thousands of acres, had received a few hundred desert acres on the borders of Pakistan by way of compensation.

Despite the ever-present danger of reprisals – by both sides – the land has been irrigated by tube wells and is blossoming as never before. The relative poverty of the refugees does not appear to affect them and they adopt a simpler way of life without any apparent difficulty. This, of course, relates to the better-off section of the refugees, but nevertheless, it has only been by sheer hard work and enterprise that these people have forged a place for themselves in the new India.

In Delhi, the enormous influx of Urdu and Punjabi-speaking Sikhs and Hindus has meant a considerable change in the balance of languages, and this has had its effect upon such unexpected things as advertisements on hoardings and in the newspapers and journals, which are produced to cater for the altered pattern of the population.

It is easy to spot the areas where refugees congregate: by the refugee shops, which are a feature of nearly every medium-sized town of north-western India. Initially, the constructions were of matting and cardboard, while the wealthier shopkeeper would have acquired some corrugated iron. In these they traded – cotton and khadi material, toys and food – and were thoroughly disliked by the established local traders. Eventually, they became part of the scenery, and Government help was forthcoming to help provide brick-built stalls for these people. But, as in every country, the trader's site is important, and having built up their reputation at a specific spot the refugee traders have shown great reluctance to move 200 yards down the road to the new buildings.

At night in Delhi one can walk for hours through rows of brightly lit stalls to discover only by daylight that the 'arcades' consisted of torn sacking supported by string. These refugee shops have now built up a fine reputation and one finds the local aristocracy, and foreigners, frequenting these shops for cloth material and saris and much else besides. Needless to say, the shopkeeper lives on the premises, for apart from having nowhere else to live, his shop is seldom staunch enough to keep out thieves. A word of advice to the would-be shopper – bargaining with these well-established stallholders will, as often as not, lead to a rebuke. Oft times one is told,

"We do not bargain here," in a superior tone, and one is presented with a ticketed article, an official-looking bill and an addition for sales tax. It is frequently so very like the procedure of home that one wonders to where the fabled and mystic East has departed.

Above, then, we have dealt with two sections of the refugee population, but there is a third section, infinitely more numerous than all the others. They live in pitiable conditions on the outskirts of towns and in those parts of the towns which are spurned by the rest of the population. They are thus the people who will be the first to be flooded out when the monsoon starts, who will go down like flies when any pestilence occurs and who display the greatest degree of poverty to be seen in India today – a city slum is always more appalling than a slum in the countryside. They do not live close to the countryside and therefore they cannot get away from the odious smells which are their constant companions, for sanitation is nonexistent. They cannot benefit from the fresh breezes that the villagers experience, and they know only the stink of their thousands of fellow refugees. They create problems for the municipalities, for they are not only a direct burden on the rates, but they also contaminate hitherto healthy areas, they increase the incidence of crime, and by such practices as 'tapping' the filtered water supply, allow entry to impurities. They do this quite simply by uncovering the mains, hammering a hole in the pipe and behold, out spurts a constant supply of water! Most of these people are unemployed and eke out a precarious existence by occasional coolie work and other menial tasks.

But at the other side of India, in Calcutta, things are different. The desolate refugees arriving at Sealdah station from East Pakistan are still to this day seeping through. They have nowhere else to go; there is no place to receive them and they merely encamp on the spot. They get off the train and subside into the station premises. They subsist virtually naked and their shelters are constructed in the station approaches, expanding into the roadway, so much so that it permits only one vehicle through at a time. The shelters are constructed of the most wretched rags, cardboard and oddments, mostly no more than three feet high. The authorities are doing their best to help the refugees; as mentioned, the shopping centres erected for refugee traders are a distinctive feature of nearly every north Indian town. In the Calcutta area, however, they merely add to the innumerable Bengalis who have to struggle hard enough as it is to get work. Moreover, the peasantry know nothing of town life; their social life disintegrates rapidly and crime becomes rampant. The West Bengal Government has done a considerable amount in resettling these people throughout the state, and just outside Calcutta many have been established on requisitioned agricultural land. The experiment is not only one of resettlement but of land consolidation and a new way of life, for the family's hut is sited on the holding itself, not grouped in villages, as for the other 99% of the countryside's population. These people are, however, the lucky ones, and indeed are the envy of many of the old-timers in the adjacent villages. But West Bengal's problem is still stupendous today and unlikely to be resolved for many years, if at all.

An interesting project has been undertaken, with more than one purpose in view, in Uttar Pradesh. If you travel from Delhi to Nanital you will pass through the Terai, which only a few years ago was a dreaded jungle area, stretching about 100 miles by 50 miles, mosquito-infested and tiger-ridden. Very few people ventured into the area except intrepid hunters of the Jim Corbett type. It was an unproductive area, but one that could be drained and cleared for farming. And that is exactly what happened – with the help of the United Nations, the Indian Government got hold of thousands of enterprising Sikhs who had come out of Pakistan. In a remarkably short time the area was cleared of jungle, the tigers retreated toward the Nepal border and the stagnant water was channelled away or put to good use in irrigation channels. With the departure of the stagnant water, the mosquitos felt obliged to depart also and the town of Rudapur was built as an administration centre, market place and workshop for agricultural machinery. Yes, agricultural machinery in India! It is amazing to find tractors working away in the huge fields. The land has been apportioned out to individual tenants, but also the great Terai State Farm takes up an enormous share of the area. Over these great tracts, farming looks more like that of the American prairies. In the area (surely the only place in India where you can get a glass of cold pasteurised milk to refresh you on your journey) dairies and cooperatives have risen, and the enterprising refugees are turning the once desolate and feared Terai into one of the most productive areas of the country.

CHAPTER 13

MAHARAJAHS

If you have not heard of any of the others, you will at least remember the rich Maharajah of Magador immortalised in that never to be forgotten ballad and who, of course, has never existed. Apart from this renowned gentleman, there happened to be approximately 500 others – Maharajas, Rajahs, Nawabs and their wives the Maharanis, Ranis and so on, and a galaxy of princes and princesses, all floating about somewhere in India – or in London's nightlife and in the huge mansions of Virginia Water.

Until a few years ago, not only were these people in existence, but their states also, and up to 1947 very many of these were lords and masters of all they surveyed. Of course, some surveyed more than others: the Nawab of Hyderabad surveyed a state nearly twice as big as England, with a population of 16 million. On the other hand, there were innumerable good souls who just about owned, and held sovereignty over, the house they lived in. Virtually none of these mucked about with any idealistic views of democracy; the thing was simply incomprehensible and they just didn't like it, and if a peasant deserved to lose his land – or his head – that was all there was to it. What purpose would be served by pushing the case through the courts, which in any event would prove expensive? The only sphere in which the British residents would get nasty was if the Maharajah's private army declared war on another state – then there may be cause to send some troops and put him back in his palace.

Let us go back a bit, remembering that it was only comparatively recently that the innumerable and tiny city states of Germany achieved ultimate unification; and it was not so terribly long ago that we had diplomatic representatives from many Italian cities in London. So, turning the centuries back, it is inevitable that we see a hotchpotch of little states in India, each claiming supreme authority and, as in any modern society, going to war with their neighbours about any odd piece of 17th century Sudetenland, as it were. The British were ruling that part of the sub-continent which had no powerful rulers who could fairly claim that they were in effective control of specific areas. And it was natural that the British should be grateful to delegate authority to these good souls in their states. Similarly, British protection was worthwhile to the rulers, and there was some incentive to keep noses fairly clean, for it was a habit of the British overlords to snaffle a slice of territory from any state that had behaved naughtily – or if the Maharajah had been just too wicked for words, he would be kicked out and told to go and live in England or somewhere equally dreadful – much the same sort of punishment as the French who sent their criminals to Devil's Island. Of course, on the other hand, if the Maharajah was particularly nice – he might have supplied troops to put down a revolt somewhere or put on a jolly good show for a visiting viceroy – then he might find himself with an extra spot of land to call his own, from which he could squeeze a few more pips.

As the years passed, the state acquired the recognition of the British Raj, and a resident pops along to join the Maharajah to accord a salute of 21 guns and to join him in whatever occupations – such as pig-sticking and any others – that the Maharajah might enjoy.

Then came the troubles of 1857 – I must be careful of terminology here, for the Indians refer to the First War of Independence, the British to the mutiny (notice the capitals and small letters, please), so let us settle for the 'troubled times', as they say in Ireland. Our loyal line was gracious enough to send some troops to the assistance of the besieged British troops in Delhi, and as a result, in grateful recognition of services rendered, was given two extra lumps of territory, which were originally British India but whose inhabitants had not been too good of late.

Things were looking up, but unfortunately Britain had not become embroiled in any more wars until that one of 1914–18, when the Maharajah sent some troops to the Middle East and donated a couple of armoured cars to the war effort at incredible expense to the state. Something misfires – perhaps it is a new morality or growing demands by Indian nationalists –

but at the end of it all, though he has almost bankrupted himself and his state, the British do not donate any more land. Instead, he is ceremoniously presented with an old field gun, carefully polished, and with a plaque from His Majesty to say, "Thanks a lot." Now this is patently unfair and annoys the Maharajah no end. So what happens? He turns nationalistic himself, and when the Viceroy is on tour, he finds himself unable to meet him. This is tantamount to treachery and in one of the squabbles with his neighbour the Maharajah of – Magador? – It is clearly time for British troops to step in and for the Maharajah to be deposed. It is all done in a gentlemanly way and he is bundled off to a beautiful house at Landsdowne, a hill station away in the far north of India.

But at this point, let us see what the Maharajah's life was like, this gent of the early 20th century, in his palace built 150 years previously. As is to be expected, the merchants, their shops and homes are crowded around their source of employment, and by the 1920s the palace, once in open fields, is in the heart of the bazaar area, though protected from it by a high wall. Facilities it had: stairs were for servants only; for the family there were slopes, up which they were pushed in sedan-type trolleys; the old fashioned punkahs, or fans, were worked by a servant who sat outside the rooms pulling a string back and forth connected to the punkah through a small hole in the door; bathrooms were lavish and water was not wanting, although, of course, it did not gush forth from taps. Electricity? Yes, a British engineer had been brought over to install a generator, which was now operated by a locally engaged member of the Maharajah's staff. It, however, frequently broke down, and some thought was being given to getting the bloke out from England again – this time to add electric fans. Throughout the private apartments the floors were covered with the most magnificent fitted carpets; and draperies were not confined to the curtains, but hung from the elaborately papered walls – a recent innovation from the west. Understandably, the walls also boasted a considerable number of photographs and paintings of the erstwhile rulers, and an odd son or two studying at Cambridge. Of pin-ups there were none, for after all, what was the point when the zenana (harem) housed so many beautiful ladies?

Perhaps one or two points about what may be delicately defined as social life would prove of interest. The Maharajah was married, an arranged marriage, of course. At the time he did not understand the term – at the age of two in fact everything was fixed up. In due course he cohabited, as the saying goes, and as his father died early, he came to the gaddi (throne) early in life. Now he had his own fancies; it is to be stated that our Maharajah was somewhat keen on the 15 to 16 age group, and on occasion he would request that a collection be rounded up for closer inspection by him for suitability for the zenana. His choice was quite pleased with herself, as it was an honour and as it was a luxurious life once she had been cleaned up and taught a few of the niceties of civilised living. Of course you are thinking, what of the poor Maharani? Well, she has a special part to play; to maintain her dignity she must assume that the zenana just does not exist – the members of it are merely maidservants. She completely ignores the fact of her husband's 'unfaithfulness'; after all, how could she have a row every time the Maharajah decides to go on the spree? In any event, she knows that it is her son who will be the first prince, who will in due course succeed to the gaddi, thereby providing her with a quiet and contented old age. In the zenana there is quite some competition for the delight of attending upon the Maharajah each night, for let's face it, the girls do not see a great deal of men and the consequences of dating outsiders are pretty dire.

Sometimes our Maharajah acts quite arbitrarily – he will send word that Miss So-and-so should be available, and the lass concerned gets a good spit and polish and perfumed for the big occasion. On the other hand, the Maharajah has curious leanings toward a more democratic approach, which is also indicative of his generous nature. On such occasions he hides a jewel somewhere in the palace and the lucky finder will be the one to nip into bed with him.

And so life in the palace progresses; unfortunately, his wife has not produced sufficient children and he feels it necessary to marry another.

This is a slight on the first wife but she is still the senior Maharani. And through all this a number of children arrive as the sons and daughters of the Maharajah. One wife has died; another is acquired in marriage. At this point there comes his deposition by the Viceroy. Our Maharajah had to leave his zenana behind; his son was placed on the gaddi in his stead, and this led to complications. For one son to accede to the gaddi, with his mother in attendance, implies that the other wives and their children are excluded. Naturally, the wives who accompanied the Maharajah into exile claimed that the other side of the family are traitors; treacherous and, later, lecherous witches who thrive on the misfortunes of their husband and father. It is not to be wondered at that when Indian independence came, all of them were in one hell of a pickle. The Indian Government disposed of the lot, giving pensions in lieu to the existing rulers, but leaving the others – the claimants or pretenders – out in the cold.

Today, those with the titles have the lolly; those without go to work like you or me, and India can today boast of princes and princesses who do fine work in public services and industry. On the side, however, they are doing all they can to get a share of the lavish pensions the rulers command, while the rulers see out their time by progressive works in their erstwhile states or have a fine time in Europe and America to relieve the monotony of pay without responsibility.

CHAPTER 14
THE VILLAGE

A very big effort was made – the more dubious members of the class were encouraged by the others and by the lecturers. The ages of the 'pupils' ranged from 25 upwards, and we were on an orientation course to teach us something of India. On this occasion we were going to undertake the adventure of adventures – a trip to a village plus a real Indian meal in real Indian style. Some acquired dysentery at the prospect; others decided on a diplomatic illness the next day; others were thrilled. In the morning our bus arrived and we began our journey, a mere 20 miles to not really a representative village, for it was in a Community Development project and therefore well advanced. Moreover, being so close to Delhi, the villagers were able to cycle into Delhi to sell their milk. They were thus a wealthy lot...

Permission had been obtained to use the canal road, or bank, and the bus trundled along until it could go no further. This is where we should have taken to the bullock cart, but nothing so menial – a huge elephant was there to take the lot of us into the village and it was prepared to operate a shuttle service. I think we would have been waiting all day for the last of the party had they not decided to walk. The intrepid climbed up onto the elephant, not by ladder but by the novel – and no doubt obvious – method of bending the animal's tail double and putting a foot in the loop!

India is a land of villages and there are half a million of them, where 80% or 90% of the population live. On the plains of India the people live in their villages, going out to tend their fields daily. There are no isolated farmhouses dotted around the countryside. It is unusual to see a single construction between the villages. The reason, historically, may be found in the need for protection, but there is an economic reason also: the Indian farmer holds a number of strips of land in different parts of the village domain; in just the same way as the peasantry of this country did hundreds of years ago before the process of land consolidation began. The arrangement is uneconomical, although it has its origin in the desire to give each villager a fair share of all the village land – good and bad. It gives rise to innumerable disputes over boundaries and the Indian Government is attempting land 'consolidation' where villagers support it.

The land, then, is dotted not with farmhouses, but with villages of mud and brick, which are sited remarkably close to one another. One wonders how the land in between them can be split up between so many people and provide all with a livelihood. The answer, of course, is that it provides not a living, but a subsistence. The English traveller will find the lack of roads remarkable and there is a complete absence of farming implements and mechanical aids.

The villages will vary in size between about 100 and 2,000 houses. The Indian villager will always denote population by the number of houses – from this it is safe to infer that the population will be five times this figure. The term house is a misnomer, for the facilities provided under this title differ radically from those expected in Western countries. But it must be said that in Indian conditions life is lived very much more outdoors than in colder parts of the world. In the home, the aim is to secure the maximum of through-draughts compatible with security and privacy – thus sayeth the Indian peasant.

The relative prosperity of a village can be judged by the proportion of brick to mud dwellings. And if one sees a two-storey building rising above the rest, perhaps whitewashed, one can assume that the village is very prosperous and that a member of the state legislature or an equally affluent son of the village has his home there. All the brick houses – plain and bare – will be flat-roofed, with the object of providing a cool yet private sleeping place for the residents.

This brings us to interpose a word – maybe a page or more – about the concept of family in India. It is confusing to talk about the joint family; it is perhaps more correct to allude to the disjointed family. As mentioned, one will find about five persons per house. This figure does not tally with what we are told of the enormous joint family, embracing grandfather and grandmother, sons and their wives, unmarried daughters, and grand-children, all residing under one roof. Joint families predominate among the wealthier sections of the village merely because they have a title to a suffi-ciently large acreage of land which will support all of them. They all work the family land and the married sons get their needful share of the produce. But even in these households one frequently finds the greatest degree of division: for 'budgetary' purposes the joint family is one, but for residential purposes the men will occupy one part of the house along with the animals and the women and children another part, with a courtyard safely separat-ing them. Indeed, this idea is frequently taken a stage further by the wealth-ier set, who can afford two homes, where the menfolk and animals occupy the second house, which is perhaps separated from the womenfolk by the village high street.

It goes without saying that there are many difficulties in the way of the young married couple getting together, and I am told that much inge-nuity is shown in this matter and frequent trips to the fields are called for. One would have thought that in this system we have a 'built-in' method of birth control!

It is amongst those lower in the social scale, including the Harijans (Untouchables) that the Western concept of family is more common, wherein the young married couple and their children live together on their own. This is a curious phenomenon, for we usually associate the more prosperous with the adoption of Western ways. Yet the reasons are clear: the poorer villagers are those who live in homes built of mud, and in a small mud hut the number of occupants is rather restricted. It is thus more frequent for the son, on mar-riage, to build another mud hut for himself and his bride, and it is quite sim-ple to do so. Moreover, the system of joint incomes does not apply so easily amongst those who are primarily engaged in the provision of services for the village, such as keeping the streets clean, working as labourers in the fields, as coolies and disposers of refuse. Their incomes are the personal rewards for each worker's services rather than the products of lands held and tilled by the whole family.

The brick houses, then, can be of one or two storeys, but mostly they are of the 'bungalow' type. In the front will be the men's room – a bare room, save for the charpoys (string beds), with an earthen floor. The animals have one side of the room reserved for them. Through this room is the courtyard, which will be shaded partially by the walls of the house and will be about the size of an average English dining room. To the rear will be the entrance to the women's room, draped with ancient calendars and with pictures of Lord Krishna and jet planes. The courtyard is the workplace of the newly arrived bride – from another village, of course – who will work alongside her mother-in-law at the household chores. Also off the courtyard will be the 'kitchen', accommodating a chula (stove), which is fuelled with charcoal and cow dung cakes and built of mud bricks. The kitchen will also house the grain store, which was filled by last season's harvest. Thus the family and the village are largely self-sufficient. I have said nothing about toilets, for there are none, and such requirements are met by visits to the fields. You will find the houses immaculately clean, which is most remarkable in view of the fact that one of the cleaning methods used is a compound of cow dung and mud. This they use to paste over the floors in a manner similar to the way we use floor polish. But the mixture has a disinfecting quality and few insects and flies are to be found on a surface treated in this way.

All this we saw on our visit and then it was time to eat. Elaborate precautions had been taken after the school children had been evacuated from their schoolhouse, and we sat down having left our shoes outside the door. A tali (tray) and dishes were produced and we sat cross-legged on mats with the floor as our table. The various dishes, meat, fish and vegetables, were put in small round dishes three inches in diameter placed in the tray. The unleavened bread – chapattis – were brought in hot (take the bottom one as it is the hottest) and the meal began. An almost frightening and embarrassed silence ensued – until one by one we got cracking with our hands and the chapatti. I have never got used to eating with my hands, although I like Indian food. The next time you eat out in an Indian village, remember that as you scoop the food up into your hand the wrist must be outward and thus above the level of the hand; try it the other way and you'll find half a pound of rice, plus curry, up your sleeve.

Let us take a look at a day in the life of one of our village acquaintances.

It is almost daybreak. The village is Nana Tika, and not one of its inhabitants boasts any alarm clock or a factory siren. But it will be light soon when the sun appears over the flat landscape and rises rapidly into the sky to give out its torrid heat, sparing none. For the time being it is pleasant – because the temperature dropped to 80°F during the night – and tattered blankets are thrown off. This is done discreetly, for we are witnessing a 'bedroom' scene enacted in the courtyard of the family of Ram Sarup. Ram Sarup is not yet up – the womenfolk are and are off out to the field, understood in this context as the ablutions, before the dawn betrays their modesty. From there to the well, which thanks to the progressive Community Development project in our village boasts a concrete wall around it so that rubbish is not blown or washed into it. Once again, modesty impels the ladies to wash with their clothes on, seldom with soap but with great vigour, which leaves the sari clinging to the figure in a most becoming manner. And as with wives at the village shop, they natter away, undisturbed by the menfolk who are gallantly dispensing with the duty of washing in order to give the lasses some privacy.

Included in the activity at the well is the process of mouth washing. The nearest approach to the Western concept is a vigorous gargle. The spitting, gargling, swallowing and choking that accompanies this ritual is almost frightening and very lengthy. It is the morning music of the East and convinces most strangers that everyone within earshot is suffering from the most malignant TB. That may be so, of course, but at the same time the westerner is all the more certain of this when he sees that they are spitting 'blood'. However, he is reassured to learn that this is the juice of the 'pan' or betel nut, which is the local chewing gum that refreshes the mouth, especially after a meal. So, much attention having been given to the throat, one wonders whether they will bother about the teeth. Indeed they do, and most Indian villagers have magnificent sets, which are daily cleaned with a piece of stick – from a branch of the neem tree they pass on their way to the well. So the lad you see hitting his goats with a big stick and jabbing inside his mouth with another (much smaller) is not really so mad after all.

Back to the ladies. Having poured water galore over each other in the impromptu shower bath, they let the sun dry them out, which it does very rapidly, and by the time they have made their way back to the house the lads have left. Pop is away without his breakfast and as he has not had one in the first 40-odd years of his life he is not going to start now just for the sake of this chapter. He is not empty handed – he is carrying his plough over his shoulder and clouting two oxen, which are reluctant to leave the comfort of Dad's bedside for the rigours of the day's work. Nevertheless, until they are squeezed out of the door it is a problem to get the other cattle out of the bedroom, where they have all passed a peaceful night. This is where son takes over – he has to take the two cattle and one buffalo, which the family possess, down to the pond to water them, and this, the kids love. For in go the animals and the children splash them and each other just for the hell of it – do you know of any children who don't like a splash in a bath tub and who are concerned with the amount of muck in the water? One adventuresome lad is keen on getting astride the buffalo as the great animal wallows, but he must be careful when the buffalo sits down! Our little chap, aged eight, is clad in nature's gift, the birthday suit, and his mates likewise. He does not go to school, although there happens to be one in the village, for his parents are not very struck on this education lark. They want to know what the purpose of it is, for nobody could be a better farmer than his Dad who never went to school. Anyway, who would look after the animals while he was away absorbing all that irrelevant book knowledge? It is, then, his job to move round the village with his three or possibly four charges, scouring for the odd piece of grass for them to eat. He stays with them so that nobody pinches them – or their milk – and to keep them off neighbours' crops. The family themselves do not drink the milk, but older brother cycles with it, in churns on the handlebars of his bike and with churns suspended behind like panniers, to Delhi 25 miles away. A little judicious watering en route enhances the amount actually sold, and the whole business is quite profitable.

Back now to Dad, who has reached what we could call patch number one. His other four patches of land are widely separated, but number one is the best land and he is, therefore, to be found much more frequently tending to this piece. Having set down from his shoulder the plough – a fragment of wood which has remained unchanged since the first day the world ever saw a plough in use, soon our farmer is at work and with a shout of "Good Morning", or rather of "Ram Ram", to his mate in the strip of land alongside his, he is away. A spot of ploughing before the sun becomes too hot, for the land must be ready for sowing when the monsoon breaks. The plough scrapes the soil as the owner urges the oxen forward with shouts and clouts, and in the still air of the warm morning, only the cries of the tillers are to be heard across the face of this roadless landscape, where seldom the sound of an internal combustion engine has been heard. And so the morning passes and by 11.30 it is just about too hot to do any more. The missus has arrived with lunch – a couple of chapattis wrapped in a cloth – and with his pitcher of water he is a made man. Sensibly, he has brought his pipe – a big edition, mind you, known as a hookah – which he sets up on the ground and encourages the smouldering coals, or rather cow dung, in the bowl of the pipe. The water through which he sucks purifies the smoke. The tree provides shade for man and beast and he slumbers on until the heat of midday slackens at about 3.30. Waking is accompanied by a few agile spits and nose clearances, which he dispenses to the four winds (which has given rise to the Indian's joke: What is the difference between an Indian and an Englishman? One blows his nose and throws it away, the other wraps it up in a cloth and puts it in his pocket).

After some colonic evacuation he gets cracking on a spot of agricultural irrigation. His sugar cane is itching for some water and it is his day to receive a supply. On the last occasion it was his turn, one of his neighbours diverted the channel and he lost half an hour of his due time because of it. So today he is watchful as he hacks away the small mound of earth that blocks the foot-wide channel and the water begins to enter his field. He knows that first the water has come from the mighty Jumna, then along a canal 80 feet wide, then along a narrower one, and so on until the earth receives back what would have been led to the sea. Sugar cane takes a lot of water and the authorities never give enough nowadays. They say that this year the Himalayan snows were not so great and so there is not so much water to be shared out to all the lands which the canals serve. Our farmer must see that each part of his crops gets a fair share, so he has sown his crops within squares about 20 feet by 20 feet, encompassed by a three or four-inch mound of soil. As one tiny plot fills with its share of the water, so he closes the inlet – merely by putting a couple of handfuls of soil in the gap – and breaking open another gap until all his land has received the life-giving liquid.

The sight of this water slowly covering the thirsty earth is something to gladden the heart. It is a very reassuring picture, and Ram Sarup sits back on his haunches, meditating on the wonder of it all. And so the evening shadows lengthen. The declining sun will evaporate little of the water, which will soon sink into the soil and do its work of nourishing the crops. The day's work is nearly done, and as darkness grows he joins others making their way back to the village and to their evening meal. In the meantime, Ram Sarup's youngster has been driving the cattle and buffalo back to the homestead.

But now we must catch up with the activities of the ladies of the household. We left them at their toilet, but back they came to the house to do just the things that any good lady would be doing in Stepney – washing, looking after the baby, expecting another, preparing the food – and gossiping with the neighbours about the latest scandal. Madam Ram Sarup will detail her daughter-in-law to make up the fire, a job frail Indira dislikes intensely, for the smoke sends one a-spluttering and makes the eyes water. But there you are; life's like that. One day she will be the senior missus in the household – but then she will be old also, which is not such a bright prospect. The grub must be prepared, the grain pounded into a flour, the chillies prepared, and inevitably more water will be required from the well, which does mean another chat before you carry the full pitcher back to the house on your head. Then the brass kitchen utensils require cleaning, with God's good earth – in the Boy Scout manner, though Indira has never heard of them, for she can neither read nor write – and then the utensils are rinsed in water. Whilst the principle is good, the hygienic aspect is not so good.

These ladies of the village are spared the joys of nappy changing, not because there is a National Health Service day nursery, but because their babies wear none. The most that any child up to five will wear is a small shirt, which is somewhat inadequate in preserving the young gentleman or lady's modesty, but labour saving. Ram Sarup's family is nothing if not progressive. They have taken to using the ambar charka, an improved spinning wheel, which Gandhi advocated, and this provides the ladies with a useful alternative to chewing their fingernails whilst gossiping.

And so the day passes for the ladies also; they have not forgotten a snooze in the heat of midday, and before she remembers where she is, the old man will be home for his supper, and woe betide her if it isn't ready!

But there is one gentleman we have not heard much about – the newly married son Sham Lal, who we mentioned was delivering milk in Delhi. He is, you might say, on shift work, for he started at 4 a.m. and got back at midday, and having had a couple of hours' nap he is away to see his mates. Today is a little special, for the Health Officer – a real, live, qualified doctor – from the Community Development headquarters is on his rounds. He is making an examination of the village children to ascertain the incidence of malaria. Dr Kapur has set out from the rest house where he is staying in order to do his tour of inspection of the nearby villages of the Community Development Block. His first stop is to be the village of Ram Lal, Nana Tika, and there being no telephone, nobody knew he was coming. Anyhow, it didn't matter. In order to undertake the hazardous work of testing for malaria, a curious assortment of tackle was felt necessary, both medical and psychological. The latter included bags of sticky sweets, with which reluctant children could be coaxed toward that big ogre, the doctor.

In the morning, Dr Kapur devoted his attention to the school children, who were dragged out of school and lined up to have their tummies felt for the swelling symptomatic of malaria. The children, on seeing his jeep's smoke – or rather dust – screen had run after it like the children with the Pied Piper of Hamelin. Dr Kapur got most of them – brothers raced home to tell the others of the booty in the form of sweets available for the feel of the tummy. But with the babies, who had to have fingers pricked and a blood sample taken, it was a little more difficult. Nonetheless, the fact that the first few did not die encouraged others to bring their babes.

And the outcome of the examinations? Dr Kapur was overjoyed, for whereas 98% had had some symptoms a few years ago, with the result that the land could not be tilled, only 2% today displayed symptoms. So that afternoon he was in jubilant mood as he went to meet the village headman (sarpanch) and his council (panchayat). Of course, not only did the council attend, but the gallery, so to speak, was packed, too, which meant that a couple of dozen people had squeezed into the tiny room, including our friend Sham Lal.

"Friends, the malaria eradication programme is virtually complete."

"Fiddlesticks" or words to that effect sayeth Sham Lal, although he wasn't even on the panchayat. Taken aback, Dr Kapur had to enquire why. And that started it.

"We have been spraying our homes diligently, but the mosquitos now seem to take no notice. They come and we can do nothing about it. Soon we will start getting malaria again."

As the evening shadows grew into night the argument went on. It was true, for one of India's most desperate needs is to eliminate the mosquito within the next few years. If not, the mosquitos that survive with their new-found immunity to the spraying will bring back the dreaded malaria and the land will go out of cultivation again, for the infected have not the energy to labour.

Yet even if the scourge of malaria is finally conquered, there still remain tuberculosis, dysentery and malnutrition, which can only be effectively eliminated by a general improvement in the standard of living. To add to their troubles, birth control practice is in its infancy – medical lecturers can get the good ladies of the village together, but when the subject of birth control is broached, they all fade away – fancy talking about such a delicate matter with a stranger! It is only with trachoma – that disease of the eyes, which eventually brings blindness – that remedial measures have any considerable success, as the menace is being successfully tackled by the authorities.

From Sham Lal's day we turn to Dad's night; the growing sugar cane is far from the village and so is in danger from marauding animals and human thieves. Ram Lal must go out again and take up position on a platform which overlooks his field. He will doze through the night with a tidy collection of stones close at hand to throw at any prowling animals and a hefty stick to beat up any attacker.

Tomorrow the cycle will be repeated.

CHAPTER 15
AT SCHOOL

When the word 'school' is mentioned, what vision springs to your mind? If you are under 40 you will probably think of a relatively modern building with its playing fields around it. Inside are desks for each child, and at certain times a break is allowed for a trip to the toilet, to drink milk or to have lunch. And after the day is over, a beneficent municipality has provided a bus to take you – and, no doubt, others – home. Now that you have been reminded of your old schooldays, kindly try to imagine yourself transferred to a land of cloudless sky and a warm sun, which is rapidly dispersing the light dew of the night. It is still early – only 7 a.m. – but along the road are groups of children, not in school uniform, but clad in very light rags, all, however, with takhties (writing boards) under their arms.

Yes, they are off to school, and they are going off early for two reasons. Firstly, there have to be two complete sessions in India's overcrowded schools, and secondly, the first classes must start early and finish early to avoid the intense heat of midday. There is no air conditioning, nor even a fan, in the shabby, brick-built construction, whose opposite number in Britain would immediately be taken for a pigsty or stable. But that is not to say that it will be dirty – the floor of baked mud will have been swept clean and the children will bring a piece of rag to sit on – on the floor, for there are no desks, no chairs, no writing books and seldom a blackboard. In short, the school is bereft of all facilities except perhaps a tattered map of India and an ABC chart – Hindi version. And in this desolate classroom, open at both ends so that any breeze will move through and give a touch of cool comfort to the pupils, classes begin. In one room, about 50 boys – or girls – will sit, at three distinct educational levels, and receive instruction from the teacher, who will be earning a modest sum per month – and no opportunity to receive 'gifts' on the side.

So, seated there, the children place their takhties, which are pieces of wood about 15 inches by 10, on their laps as they sit cross-legged on the floor. Their parents, having invested four pence for each of these boards, must see that they are used. For the equivalent of half a farthing, a piece of bamboo sharpened at one end is purchased, which is used for writing. Writing with a crude ink, they learn their Hindi alphabet and learn to count by their hieroglyphics on the takhti, and when they fill up their board with figures, they use a white chalk to obliterate what they have written and start again. Writing will be followed by arithmetic, arithmetic by general knowledge – "Who is our Prime Minister?" "When did we win independence?" "What is the capital of India?" – and the answers will be recited in unison.

It is strange but true that there is an amazing degree of self-sufficiency in these schools. Appalling though the paucity of resources is, by Western standards, these primary schools of India want for little. For example, the intrusion of desks would make the accommodation situation impossible. Moreover, the children, used to squatting in the home, would learn a way of sitting alien to them and make for difficulties in social relations within their families. Likewise with books and writing materials: their cost would be prohibitive to the Indian Exchequer and accustom the children to a facet of life which bears no resemblance to everyday affairs. Yet at the same time there is an enormous amount of work to be done in order that all Indian children – instead of only 50% – can enjoy these meagre facilities. It is a field in which private groups of Europeans and their organisations can do a great deal, and at very little cost, and be assured of a great welcome for their efforts.

Let me tell you the story of one of these schools. It was in Delhi that the idea first found its expression. There were few of this particular organisation's employees' children going to school – the schools were overcrowded, too far away and the private schools too expensive. So about a hundred children between the ages of six and 12 learnt nothing and devoted their surplus energies to activities of a 'junior teddy-boy' type. These were the children of employees earning under £12 a month – drivers, messengers, cleaners, personal servants – and who were housed in a compound close to their place of work. With a large tent, which was hired for the sum of 15 shillings per month, some rejected coconut matting from the offices and with an English-speaking teacher the school began operations.

The school's income was derived from the children – Rs 6 per month from each child – plus donations from the Europeans. Outgoings per month were £4 to the teacher (who also received the monthly fees of each of the 50 children) and the hire of the tent. With this meagre budget, education was provided for the children, who learn English and Geography in addition to the three Hindi 'Rs'. Sitting on the ground, 30 little girls and 20 boys get on with the job of learning. On arrival, the teacher stands them all to attention and inspects for cleanliness – behind the ears, under the nails, in the hair – and woe betide those who arrive in dirty clothes. They are copying Western concepts of curriculum now – modelling and arts and crafts. Clay dolls are made by the girls from the mud of the Jumna River, collected by the teacher, and baked in the sun. Coloured paper – scrounged or rejected by the memsahibs – provides the clothes. And they make birds with heaven knows what and houses with matchboxes suitably daubed with mysterious dyes. Their models are based on their own way of life; their own huts; the implements used in cooking; the wells from which they draw their water.

And under the guidance of their first-rate teacher, dancing is taught – Indian style, of course – and the boys play the musical accompaniment, squatting on the floor with the drums as the girls move with the wonderful gestures of the Indian dance. But things in this world never go smoothly – there are the demands of Muslim parents for their children to learn Urdu; the complications of religious holidays, plus those thrown in by the presence of their European employers; of the children who have won prizes and those who have not, and of the goondas, or ne'er-do-wells, who try to intimidate the teacher in his good work. The children, however, are learning; idleness is replaced by creative activity, even though the school occasionally has to be hastily dispersed whilst a snake is extracted from under the coconut matting, or postponed whilst the heavy monsoon rains drain from the flooded school. And once the school is going, there are others to help – United Nations bodies provide sufficient dried milk for a glass of milk to be given to each child daily and add a special nourishing biscuit or two. And some health organisation offers to do TB vaccination. All of this does wonders for the children and helps to fight the malnutrition which deludes so many Europeans into exclaiming, "Aren't they good; aren't they quiet!" as they sit so placidly at their lessons. What they do not realise is that their poverty means a lack of a balanced diet and their stamina is short-lived. This lack of stamina was a big problem when anything resembling a sports' day was organised. Care had to be taken to ensure that the strenuous activities were liberally interspersed with spells of more leisurely activities.

Where do the children go after their 6-rupee-a-month education? It would be nice to be able to report that the organisation was running a secondary school and university college! The opportunities for employment are few – the older ones, with their fathers' help, aim to get work as messengers or servants in the same company, and will be deeply satisfied if they can aspire to something over Rs 100 per month without having to undertake the agonies of manual labour in a country as warm as India.

CHAPTER 16
THE WORKERS

The economist will remind you of three elements of the building industry: capital, employee and entrepreneur. In this none too accurate, but somewhat representative, account of the industry in India, we will assume the availability of the first requirement – capital. We will forget about the existence of mighty cranes, bulldozers, immaculate scaffolding, lifts for materials and the like. Instead, in front of an embryonic luxury hotel – as indeed it turns out to be – there is a confused mass of knobbly wooden scaffolding (I can think of no suitable phrase to describe the hotchpotch of unshaped branches and bits of trees that serve as scaffolding) which blocks out sight of the building. Add to this a horde of building labour, both men and women, as ants on an anthill and you have a fairly typical building site.

But let us look closer; an extensive and self-contained township has been built in order to house the workers who have come to build this structure. It is a mass of brick-built huts – brick precariously balanced on brick, without the superfluous luxury of a spot of cement in between. The four walls – or rather three and a half, allowing for an entrance – support a piece of matting for roofing, or for those in the super-tax class, a piece of corrugated iron. Clearly, such employees want for little; an enterprising storekeeper has set up shop – very quickly, for once again it needs only a few bricks, some cardboard packing cases and a charpoy (bed) to cater for the wants of the temporary community. It behoves us, as in the inspection of all new towns, to discuss facilities with the housewife, who no doubt is busily preparing the midday meal and looking after baby. But no – there are no housewives to be seen; perhaps we are in the bachelors' section, or perhaps they are at the bazaar. We cannot find them, for they are working with their husbands in a family group. The contractor employs them as a group and the Government lays down a standard wage and daily hours. But it is not wise for the worker to make detailed reference to that statute to his employer!

So there they are – the ideal happy family; never parted by work or in play. And, of course, baby is with them. Whilst the five-year-olds play precariously on the unfinished eighth floor of the building, baby swings contentedly in a hammock of old sari cloth between two girders as Mum transports endless baskets of cement on her head from ground level to the tenth floor. Mother is a Rajasthani – those magnificent women, who in their groups going to and from work are to be seen in the vicinity of any building site in the early morning or late afternoon. They make a fine sight, clad in their red skirts and blouses, baby on hip and singing without a care in the world on £3 a month.

And now let us turn to the kingpin of the project – the contractor himself. He will probably be a Sikh who drives an eight-year-old American car (none entered the country after that time because of import restrictions, and he can't wangle a licence to import), and in theory he also should not have a care in the world. He does not have to bother with trade unions, and after all, he only has to put in an appearance at his site office once or twice a day and sit in semi-darkness whilst an employee flings water on the matting that covers the window and door in an effort to keep the lord and master cool. He has parked his car in the shade of the only tree available, which was rapidly vacated by two of his workers having their 'elevenses'. But let us not be under a misapprehension, for his worries are great: there is a cement shortage and it is rationed; his overheads are mounting, for 'backhanders' to be paid to ensure that his constructions will pass the inspector are large. I was told of one contractor who determined to 'go straight' and not to give the inspectors their 'gifts'. After he had to demolish one side of the building six times as it allegedly did not come up to specification, he gave up. And as the attempt had knocked him back financially, he erected the seventh wall with sub-standard materials, which was approved, and within three months the building had collapsed!

At the end of it all, however, a building emerges; there is an end to the clamour and activity. The colourful red garments and their wearers leave their homes, which are razed and replaced by a lawn, immaculately tended and watered. The visitors to the new hotel would never believe that where they sit under the sun umbrellas an enterprising shopkeeper sold his wares.

But this is not the only building procedure known in India. For a more up-to-date method we must visit the Mecca of 20th century man. It is close to a Sikh temple, a beautiful place called Anandpur Sahib, set on a mound near the foot of the Himalayas. However, we are not bound for this temple and we move on, with the open road ahead, without anything to show that close by lies the pride of India. Instead, one is driven to despair by the lack of construction – not even in fences has there been any 'capital investment'; there are no solid buildings, apart from a few brick houses in some villages, but these are more reminiscent of hastily erected outhouses. Suddenly, one encounters a canal – yes, a brand new one – and further on a town a mere ten years old; a new town resembling a large encampment of army huts without fences. In this live the thousands who work on the great dam and hydro-electric works of Bhakra-Nangal. The township is some miles from the works, and as one enters the area, cameras are taken and you 'sign in'. It is an immense project which aims to regulate the supply of water to the plains and to irrigate much of the desert land of Rajasthan. Electricity is a by-product. Thousands of villagers have had to be resettled.

The mighty enterprise is run by an American, who, it is said, controls operations from a semi-circular desk covered with telephones, one of which is white and marked 'Nehru', which is a direct line to the Prime Minister's office 200 miles away in Delhi. The project is spectacular; it is visible; it is picture-worthy; and it is symbolic of the vigour of the new India. Therein lies much of its value, for there is something different at Bhakra-Nangal. It is the degree of mechanisation – there are no hordes of workers and none of the multitudinous clamour that accompanies building operations elsewhere in India. There are no children playing about, nor hammocks with their baby occupants slung in the shade of the structure-to-be.

In contrast to the highly mechanised and American administered project of Bhakra-Nangal, we have the Chambal River development further south close to the dacoit areas. Here, on the borders of Rajasthan and Madhya Pradesh, another dam is being built without all the accompanying paraphernalia of mechanisation; the crane which lifts huge quantities of materials to the building point a hundred or more feet high is replaced by a multitude of Rajasthani women with tiny quantities of sand and cement in baskets on their heads. They walk in single file up inclined scaffolding and deposit their burden at the top. They are the Irish of North India – from the semi-desert of Rajasthan – and they move, complete with family, to the big projects in town and country. They are also the aristocrats of the Indian working class, for all members of the family are earning and later they will be able to retire and buy land with their savings.

It is claimed by many that these non-mechanised projects are cheaper, in Indian conditions, and of course they provide work for many more people than is possible by mechanised methods. But because this controversy does exist, clearly the margin of advantage, one way or the other, is not great. However, the social advantage in giving work to so many is of great importance, even though it withdraws the population from their traditional modes of life. Meanwhile, India advances, the water and electricity produced nourish the fields and the country's economy, and a further step in India's progress is marked – not noticeably so, but of significance nonetheless.

No visitor to India should leave the country without a visit to one of these sites – there is something for everyone: for the amateur sociologist; the economist will find interest; the architect and engineer will marvel at the magnificent constructions that emerge from such apparent disorganisation; the artist will be enthralled by the rhythm and harmony in movement of the women passing bricks by hand as they catch them, turn their bodies and throw them one by one along the line to the point where they are to be used; and it is a photographer's paradise.

I wonder what the future will hold for these workers and their country. Let me return later.

Wood for the funeral pyre. Nepal.

The last journey. Kathmandu.